THE LIFE BRIDGE
YOUR JOURNEY FROM AN UNCONSCIOUS TO A CONSCIOUS LIFE

BY ULRIK NERLØE

Copyright © 2017 By Ulrik Nerløe

All rights reserved. No part of this book may be used or reproduced in any manner whatsoever without prior written consent of the authors, except as provided by the United States of America copyright law.

Published by Best Seller Publishing®, Pasadena, CA
Best Seller Publishing® is a registered trademark
Printed in the United States of America.
ISBN: 978-1-946978-52-3

This publication is designed to provide accurate and authoritative information with regard to the subject matter covered. It is sold with the understanding that the publisher is not engaged in rendering legal, accounting, or other professional advice. If legal advice or other expert assistance is required, the services of a competent professional should be sought. The opinions expressed by the authors in this book are not endorsed by Best Seller Publishing® and are the sole responsibility of the author rendering the opinion.

Most Best Seller Publishing® titles are available at special quantity discounts for bulk purchases for sales promotions, premiums, fundraising, and educational use. Special versions or book excerpts can also be created to fit specific needs.

For more information, please write:
Best Seller Publishing®
1346 Walnut Street, #205
Pasadena, CA 91106
or call 1(626) 765 9750
Toll Free: 1(844) 850-3500

Visit us online at: www.BestSellerPublishing.org

PREFACE

One afternoon in August 2009 I picked up my son, Christopher, from school. He had just started school and was almost 6 years old. It had been a hard and challenging day. It felt as though nothing had gone right for me all day long. I was stressed, and was, I have to admit, in a pretty bad mood. All the way from work to my son´s school, I could feel what a lousy day it had been and how much it was affecting me. I decided to try not to let it ruin my mood and instead focus on being with Christopher. I was tired and had run out of energy, but tried to pull myself together before I arrived at the school.

When I met Christopher in the schoolyard, I smiled and put on a happy face. Like I had everything under control like the SUPER Dad I wanted him to see me as. I could see how happy he was to see me, when we met up in the schoolyard.

Little did I know that, only minutes after we got into the car, my life would change forever. That my life would be turned upside down, and nothing would ever be the same after that day.

After we had driven 2-300 meters from the school, my wonderful little boy said these words to me:

"Dad, I´ve been thinking about something. Don´t you think it´s about time you stopped being mad at yourself, so you can stop being mad at the rest of us all the time?"

Time and place stood still. Completely still. I almost drove off the road, yet all at once, for the first time in my life, I saw clearly the path my life was destined to follow. Everything and nothing made sense all at the same time. I was completely silent. What I really wanted to do was break down sobbing with joy and sorrow, but instead I just sat there in silence. The feeling of being pinned against a wall – caught out – was overwhelming.

It couldn´t have been more than a few seconds that passed but, for me, they felt like years. But I managed to answer him:

"Sweetheart, you know I think you´re right!" and Christopher answered, "I think it might be a good idea anyhow!"

A 5-year-old child – so wise about life at such a young age. Me, stripped of all pretence. All my convictions. All those "Dad of the Year" aspirations down the drain, and yet it was one of the most beautiful moments of my life. In that instant, I realized that my son, Christopher, had been sent to me as a gift. A soul sent through love to help me live my life, not just now, but for the rest of my days.

Had it not been for my son and his gift, you wouldn´t be sitting here now reading this book.

This was the beginning of my new life. The life I am living now and will live for as long as I breathe. The journey which began that day is a journey without end. A journey of growth which has led me to many places in my life, and will lead to many more. Not only physically, but just as much in terms of understanding.

My own personal journey has made me stop and take stock of things. It made me put my life on hold and ask myself some very fundamental questions. Questions and answers that I will address in this book. A process which, incidentally, has made me realize that almost all the dreams I have had in life have come true.

The process that I refer to is "The Life Bridge". It is a way of viewing your life that allows you to simultaneously embrace your dreams and make them come true, while you fully experience the special joys that surround you today. That's the process that I unconsciously have been through and it is the process I would like to help you become conscious about.

When my life took this unexpected turn, I realized what an enormous difference this has made to me. How things in my life made much more sense, became more meaningful, if you like. How much happier I became. I discovered what it actually means to feel happy, and was much more conscious of whether I *was* happy or not. I understood the importance of making active choices, or conversely, of actively opting out, no matter what aspect of life this involves. It was partly this, among other things, that made me decide to work with people today. I take people on the same journey that I have been on, and am still on.

Today, I surround myself with people I want to be with, and who want to be with me. I don´t waste resources on people who only want to be a part of my life on certain conditions. It may sound a little glib, but I only work with those I want to work with. I would rather turn down the opportunity to work with someone if it doesn´t feel right to me. How do I know that? I know it because one of the things my journey has taught me is to trust my intuition 100%. This helps me make the right decisions every day. This is one of the things I am going to teach you in this book.

When you are happy, you become energized. I am convinced that the key to everything is energy. It is what drives the universe. No petrol in the car – no transport. No energy in the body – no heartbeat. No energy in life – no happiness in life. Energy is everything, and energy is also magnetism. An ability to attract the elements you would like to have in your life. This not only applies to the things you dream about but also, to an equal degree, to the people you would like to be a part of your life.

I feel enormously privileged to have those I have, around me in my life. My wonderful wife who is my rock, my ultimate sparring partner and my guiding light when I sometimes lose focus. My remarkable children, Maria and Christopher. Christopher, the quiet observer who delivers mind-blowing messages with tremendous modesty and Maria, who is just as much a gift in her own way. A beautiful soul who was put in this world to teach me that I don´t have to be right all the time. Don´t always have to have the last word and, by questioning my habits and convictions, also challenges them. My lovely girl, a real creative, "out of the box" thinker, also possesses another gift. She is one of the most empathic people I know.

My family, my wonderful friends, who are there through thick and thin, despite the fact that living and breathing my dream, leaves me with precious little time to spare. In spite of all this, we still love and care for each other, and for that, I am deeply grateful.

Attracting only the people you really want in your life, also means that you are sometimes given the opportunity to meet unique individuals. People who help make us the people we are, what we are, and why we are just what we are. It is these people who supply the jigsaw pieces of the puzzle that makes up our life. Pieces that when connected help us move forward to achieve what we dream of.

Michael, my best friend and business partner. You are always there for me, helping me to reach my, and our, goals and dreams. You provide the balancing influence that helps make those dreams happen by turning "ideas on the run" into reality. You have contributed incisive and valuable insights throughout the process from start to finish, and have made sure that the knowledge I take for granted makes sense to other people, too.

In January 2013, my nephew, Erik, moved to Denmark from Barcelona. A bright young man willing to give it a chance in a new country. 18 years old and full of confidence – without really having any idea of what he could do here. Erik started working for me. Gradually, he became a big part of my daily life. We worked together on my journey and the development of my company "Unified People". He became my sparring partner, my reality check, my extended arm, my extra pair of legs, the one who looked out for me, and above all, my travel companion. Erik set off on an inner journey of his own. To gain an understanding of who he is. He set out on a process that would help him begin to understand what it means to be human, and thus how he could get the most out of life.

Time after time, Erik showed me that when you follow your intuition and work with it, you will succeed. It was, therefore, not difficult decision to make when, in the fall of 2016, I asked Erik if he would consider co-writing this book with me. A task which involved him helping to document and describe the knowledge which we had collected over a period of almost 7 years.

Had it not been for Erik´s huge contribution during the past 12 months, this book would not have seen the light of day so quickly. For that I am deeply grateful. Thank you from the bottom of my heart, Erik, for putting *your* heart and soul into realizing my dream.

My dear old artist friend, Henrik, who has helped me out creating the most beautiful illustrations for this book. Not only have you created the most magical paintings for my house and office but now you have also added your magical touch to my first book. That I am so gratefull for.

Christine, how funny it is how time can work for us and connect us. Knowing you since I was a child and now you have helped me out to realize a big dream by translating this book into English. I am so grateful for your patience with me and for the strong enthusiasm you have had for the first second of creating the book.

Last but by no means least, life led me to cross paths with a very special person. A person who, from the very beginning, intuitively knew what I was trying to accomplish with this book, and could understand and "interpret" my disorganized and, at times, extremely abstract thoughts so they could be converted into text that made sense. Julie, you are a star- my guiding light- and a true wordsmith who has worked incredibly hard to get my message across in this book. You are both pure of soul and crystal clear in your understanding of what the essence of this message is, when at times it must have seemed so complex. This has provided us with a solid basis during the process of writing this book. Working with you has been an enriching experience, and one in which I feel we have learned from each other.

And now to YOU – dear Reader. I hope that this book will inspire you to take some "time-out" in your life.

Get your act together and take a look at your life! Use this book and its messages to create the life you would really like to have. If you do, you will be playing your part in helping to make tomorrow's world a better place – for all change starts with ourselves.

NOTHING COMES FOR FREE

As you read this book, you might be tempted to think, "It´s alright for Ulrik. He is obviously one of those people who was born under a lucky star, or with a silver spoon in his mouth."

But this is where you´d be wrong. Here´s where you´ll either be disappointed or inspired! Everything I have achieved in life, I did on my own.

When I got that wake-up call from my son in August 2009, I realized that my time in the IT industry was drawing to an end. It was clear to me that freedom was what I desired above all else. I was 100% convinced that starting my own business was the way to go. I had lots of good ideas, but too many good ideas are not always a good thing. It makes it hard to choose the right ones. Which one is best?

One thing, however, was clear to me. I wanted to make a difference. At the back of my mind, I had always dreamt of making a difference to as many people´s lives as possible. So this is where I started.

I gradually began to realize that throughout my career I had always tried to influence the management´s mindset and their way of working in the companies in which I had been employed. I could see that almost all of those companies made the same mistakes. The management style they practiced made their employees feel taken for granted, and this had a hugely negative effect on the whole company culture. Many of these people felt as if they were simply a cog in the wheel of an automated machine in some factory. Their work meant nothing to them. There was not a trace of human values, passion or inspiration to be found. Just a machine that was expected to run faster and faster with every day that passed.

It was this general trend that was the inspiration for the concept I created. A concept of creating change. A concept that would improve people's daily lives – both at work and at home – and ultimately, make the world a better place starting from right now.

If you don't enjoy your work, you will take this home with you and vice versa. It's also a fact that happy people perform much better than unhappy people. Those who are inspired, however, can create pure magic. The concept behind my dream of creating Unified People was to start a popular movement that would help inspire others to free themselves from the limitations put on them, and achieve a magical level of energy. This would not only benefit them, and enrich their families, but the companies they worked for would profit from it, too.

During my four years as chairman of the board of our children's daycare center, I tried out some of my simpler theories and assumptions. I could see what a big difference these made to the employees, the children and, not least of all, the parents. It was already a wonderful daycare center to start with, with extraordinarily talented staff, 100% dedicated to their work. In spite of this, it was clear to everyone that implementing my philosophies would inspire those who worked there even more.

It was this experience, among others, that made me start "Unified People" in February 2011.

Against all odds, I threw myself into it. I had complete faith that the world would welcome me with open arms. I was confident that we would be a success from day one – even though our concept was brand new. It didn't take long before I could see that I would need a hand with the day-to-day operations. As fate would have it, a very competent woman who had served on the board with me, expressed interest in joining the company. Together, we began to develop the concept and present it to potential clients. Many expressed great interest in our concept and our ideas.

There was just one small problem. Although most people thought it was good, NOBODY wanted to buy it. We held meeting after meeting. Mustered all the enthusiasm we could, only to be rejected once more. We knew we could make a difference – not only to the organizations we visited, but also to their top and bottom lines. None of these companies were focusing on development. All of their focus was on surviving. Month after month passed. The pattern repeated itself over and over again, but no revenue materialized, until finally I was forced to make a hard decision and let my terrific partner go. A great loss, but a necessary one.

I was under pressure from all sides. I was afraid. I struggled to keep believing in it, but found it difficult to hide my fears. All I was attracting was negativity and thus more fear. Things started happening fast after that as we slid into a situation that just got worse and worse. In the past 10 months, we hadn't earned a single dollar. We had been up and running for 16 months. Our turnover represented just 15% of our operating profit. Money was pouring out of the company, just to keep us afloat. Including the bank's money. With the benefit of hindsight, I can see that although I thought I was doing everything I could during this period, I was actually making things worse. Destroying more than I created.

In September 2012, the bank called a halt to everything. They gave me 6 months to pay off 50% of my debts, those we had incurred setting up and running United People. If I couldn't, they would force us to sell our house. My life stood still. I was about to lose everything it had taken years to create. I had clung on to my dream, but had sacrificed EVERYTHING to achieve it. The worst-case scenario that I had never thought would happen was now about to become a reality. Everything rational turned irrational within seconds. We were so close to our goal, yet so far away. Both my wife and I could sense that it was only a matter of months, or even weeks, before our venture would succeed, but I was paralyzed with fear.

The problem was that I hadn´t realized just *how* very afraid I was until a dear friend asked me, "Ulrik, what are you so afraid of? Why are you clinging on, instead of letting go and being who you are?"

It dawned on me then that I had been pretending to be something I wasn´t at all. That I had absorbed a lot of negative impressions of how I thought I SHOULD be. Patterned my behavior on that of those around me – instead of revealing my authentic self. Instead of remaining 100% true to what I felt was right. Instead of believing that there was a place for my views and philosophy in this world.

Of course, this insight didn´t mean that my fears vanished overnight. But it was a new start, and did change the way things turned out.

A few days later, I had a session with my mentor, whose wise guidance helped me to see things more clearly and get rid of my negative energy. After I had cried for an hour, I was asked to repeat a few words which turned out to be ones that transformed the rest of my life. These words were:

"I command ALL negative energies that do not belong to me to leave my body now and forever in the name of the Universe."

I had to repeat this sentence out loud over and over again- for at least 30 minutes – which I did.

When I arrived back at my office, my phone rang. It was the CEO of a client we had done some work for 16 months previously. He was calling with a job for me which would require being there 3 days a week for the next 12 months. A job that involved working on their strategy which could turn my situation around 360 degrees. As we were finishing our conversation, I could see that I had another call coming in, so we wrapped things up and I took the other call. It was another client requesting a number of workshops that he felt could make a difference to his company. While I was talking to this client, an email ticked in from a third client who wanted to hold a course on strategy. An hour later, a fourth mail arrived from a CEO who wanted to start up a mentoring course.

In just 6 hours my world had been turned upside down. Everything went from darkness to light. All my fears were transformed into hope and faith. It was the start of my new life. The start of a new ending that would allow freedom to become the cornerstone of my future – the foundation on which dreams could be created, and dreams could turn into reality.

The "scars" I was left with from that period were transformed into knowledge. I learned to be grateful for everything in life. We attract what we feel and think, and if we think negatively and are filled with fear, then that is what we will end up with. On the other hand, if we let go of our negativity and follow our guiding light, then we can get through even the most awful periods and come out stronger and renewed on the other side.

I have always loved the fairy tale, "The Ugly Duckling", and that period in my life has merely confirmed why that fairy tale in particular has always meant so much to me.

TABLE OF CONTENTS

Preface iii

Chapter 1: Introduction 1

Chapter 2: What Are Your Dreams? 13

Chapter 3: How Do You Prioritize? More About
Unconscious And Conscious Choices 25

Chapter 4: Insight Provides Perspective 37

Chapter 5: You Have A Choice. Now. 45

Chapter 6: On Habits – And How We Break Them 51

Chapter 7: The Plaster Effect 57

Chapter 8: The Head Vs. The Heart 61

Chapter 9: Listen To Your Heart 67

Chapter 10: It Is Time To Recap – Have You
Already Become A Little More Conscious? 75

Chapter 11: The Authentic Self 81

Chapter 12: Use Your Intuition 85

Chapter 13: What Is Energy? 91

Chapter 14: The Life Bridge Model 101

Chapter 15: The Path To Visualization 109

Chapter 16: The Universe Is Listening 115

Hapter 17: What You Should Know About Time 119

Chapter 18: The Power In Asking For Help 125

Chapter 19: Connecting The Dots 129

Chapter 20: Everything Is Connected 133

Chapter 21: You Can Move The Process Along 139

Chapter 22: Let'S Call It The "Principle" Of Attraction 143

Chapter 23: To Conclude 151

Questions/ Exercises 157

CHAPTER 1
INTRODUCTION

"Every morning you have
two choices: Continue to sleep
with your dreams or
wake up and chase them."

Carmelo Anthony

WHAT IS "THE LIFE BRIDGE"?

WHAT DO WE MEAN BY "FROM UNCONSCIOUS TO CONSCIOUS LIVING?"

I am not going to beat around the bush here. Let´s tackle it head on right from the start with no reservations….

You´re probably sitting there wondering whether "The Life Bridge" could be the answer to many of the questions you have about your life. About whether it might be the wake-up call you need – a nudge in the right direction. About whether it could change your life. Provide happiness. If it could make all your dreams come true.

The short answer is YES.

"The Life Bridge" will help you attain a higher level of awareness about all the things you cherish and value in your life right now - instead of taking them for granted. "The Life Bridge" will lead you to a deeper, conscious understanding about what you dream of accomplishing, and what you wish for in your future.

What kind of feelings would you like to experience every day? Which of your attitudes matter most to you, and would stimulate you to give your best in your day-to-day activities? What goals would you like to see fulfilled in the future? "The Life Bridge" will teach you to balance the your focus and energy between the present you cherish now, and the future you desire

And I can promise you this. When you reach that point, where you achieve this insight, you will notice elements in your life that you have previously overlooked. Elements that are constantly evolving and which you yourself can influence to add meaning to your life, now and in the future.

So far, so good! That more or less summed up the short version. Here, in the following chapters, you can read the more detailed explanation. What they contain will change your life and make your dreams come true.

Are you ready? Good. Then let´s begin.

WHAT CAN YOU LEARN FROM MY OWN PERSONAL JOURNEY?

It was only 2-3 years ago that I first realized that almost all of the dreams I had had during my life up until then, had actually come true, without my really realizing up until that point, exactly why. For me, of course, it has been a very long journey, one which has had more than its fair share of challenges and hard knocks along the way, but one which has basically been filled with the kind of things we all go through in life, the challenges and events we perhaps do not examine too closely or reflect upon at the time.

My journey of growth started at the beginning of my career when I was just 21-22 years old, when I started off in the IT industry, after having spent 5 years in the fashion retail business which I had enjoyed very much, and had done well in.

I found myself thrust into the world of IT which is tough, cold and cynical, but where business was booming. I was working for a large American concern that was growing fast. What could be more exciting for a young person than getting a foot in the door of this exciting world, earning big money and living life in the fast lane, all of which blinds you to the fact that you are gradually losing, not only your own sense of self-worth, but also the ability to control the direction in which you are heading.

During the 12-13 years in which I worked in the IT industry, I felt, quite frankly, invincible- a world champion. Sales competitions? Not a big deal, I was usually one of the winners. I was frequently chosen for promotion. I more or less wrote my last three employment contracts myself. I was headhunted anywhere from 1-4 times a week. I was a star. I earned a great deal of money, had my pick of top-of-the-range cars, and bought the house I desired. To all outward appearances, most people would have said that I was a happy man, with the perfect life. I thought so, too. I basked in the glow of this privileged environment, together with my equally successful colleagues, and strove to live up to their perception and expectations of me.

But the fact was that there came a day when it hit me, that although I was making a good living in the IT industry, I hated every minute of it. Everything that was important to me, my core values such as empathy, honesty, respect, my sense of ethics and morality, were gradually getting harder and harder for me to spot.

And it was then that my world began to change, little by little. Right then and there, I began to connect with my own personal values again. I began to understand what was really important to me. I began to admit to myself that what I had been doing for the past 10 years was no longer the right way forward for me. Suddenly, I found myself at the point of no return on this journey. There was no way back. I began to look inwards. Ask questions. I began to rediscover my inner love for myself, my inner freedom. I found the key to turning my life around. It was quite simply magical.

And, in fact, this is exactly what this book is about. About guiding you towards the path that will help you change your life. Helping you recognize your own core values. Your authenticity. About helping you to learn how to listen to who YOU are. To what makes YOU happy. About helping you get *in touch* with yourself. It is about helping you to reconnect with yourself so that you can actually feel what is happening to you from the neck down! It is about creating a balance between the mind and the soul. It is about helping you to understand that it is not "the sky that is the limit, but your mind that is the limit". In principle, most of your dreams can be fulfilled, if you just follow a special system that provides the key to attracting your dreams.

WHAT DO YOU DREAM OF?

But first, let´s start somewhere else entirely. By asking ourselves: "What do I dream of?"

When you ask people today, "What do you dream of?" their instinctive response is usually something like financial freedom, to win the Lottery, to travel around the world, etc. There are numerous suggestions, but they all have the same thing in common. And during my many – hundreds, if not thousands of mentoring hours – speaking to people about their dreams, I have reached the conclusion that dreams are, above all, based on the concept of freedom.

We all dream of that feeling of being free. Whether it is to be free of financial worries, or a sense of "emotional" freedom. The ability to be able to actively choose to participate or not, is the thing which the majority of us dream of.

INSIGHT PROVIDES PERSPECTIVE

The problem is, however, that by the time we reach that moment of realization, and call a halt to things, it is often already too late, or at the very least, late enough to cause us grief in some way. Usually, we only stop once we hit a wall.

In 2000, I suffered a blood clot in the heart which knocked me out completely for two months. Nevertheless, I returned to the hectic lifestyle I had led before the blood clot incident, as if nothing had happened. I had learned nothing from it.

That naive approach, that lack of insight, the failure to understand what my body was trying to teach me, the failure to recognize what my soul was desperately trying to make my mind see, passed me by completely until I went down with stress and was forced to take sick leave some years later. This time, both my body and soul were clamoring for attention. For help. This time, the message was clear – that if I didn't LISTEN, next time I would be dead.

Although frightening, this period of sick leave proved to be a turning point, because some of the people treating me began to ask me some basic questions, to which I found myself unable to answer. Questions such as:

"What really makes you happy?", "Who are you?""What do you take for granted?", "What does the word energy mean to you?"

I began to reflect on my life. How conscious am I about the things I do? The way I think, the way I choose to live my life? And how many of these things, do I do unconsciously?

These questions, and the answers to them, launched me on a journey that has now lasted for 10 years. In this book, I would like to share with you these questions, and the answers I found. For I have experienced myself how these questions and answers have quite simply transformed my life. It has been a magical journey. Yes, what I have learned, in fact, is that life itself is wondrous, and almost anything is possible if you learn to ask the right questions and search for the right answers.

WHAT YOU THINK IS WHAT YOU ATTRACT

When we think big, we get big. Think small, and that's what you'll get. Think positive, and you'll receive a positive reaction, but think negative and you'll attract the negative. But what does this actually mean? In practice, it means that, to a great degree, we are able to shape the life we desire. It is up to you to decide what day you would like to start your week on, and when you would like it to finish. How you would like your day to start, and how you would like it to finish.

An awful lot of people think there is nothing worse than a Monday morning. So when they leave for work their energy is low. Their motivation is at rock bottom. The only thing they think about all day is getting through Monday so Tuesday can start! They have basically already decided, and accepted, that Mondays are awful. Period. But who decided that in the first place? Who told you that? Who taught you that Mondays are doomed to be awful? And who can turn this situation around so Monday could actually turn out to be a good day?

THE DREAM OF FREEDOM

An awful lot of people play the Lottery. Why do we play the Lottery? Because we dream of winning a lot of money to buy us more freedom in our lives.

The term "freedom" is one of my favorite expressions. For the term "freedom" does not necessarily have to mean money. I could sit on a park bench anywhere in the world and feel like the world's richest man in terms of freedom, without it costing me a cent. I could also, of course, do something else that involved spending money which would give me the same sense of freedom. But for me personally, the concept of "freedom" does not necessarily relate to having a lot of money. The mistake we make is in deciding that money equals freedom. Naturally, some people will reject this argument and say, "That's all very well, but money *does* buy you greater freedom."

And yes, of course, that is true, depending on how you want to live your life. And obviously, we have to go to work in order to pay the rent. But, in my opinion, it is a very big mistake to think that that we will have a much greater sense of freedom if only we have enough money.

Throughout my life, I have always "thought big", dreamt big, and while I was growing up, when I talked about those dreams, my father always said to me, "Ulrik, stop building castles in the air." or "Ulrik, forget all those pipe dreams! Those kind of things don´t happen to people like us. We´ve never won so much as a nickel in a magazine competition!" I never really got what he meant by that. In any case, it didn´t work, as I continued to dream big and, what´s more, was successful in making almost all of my dreams come true. So the good news is that using this book, I am going to teach you how to make almost all of your dreams a reality. I will teach you how to become aware of the kind of life you really want, the one you dream of unconsciously perhaps.

WHEN DO WE SAY "ENOUGH IS ENOUGH"?

Today, when I look at where I am now, and look back at who I was then, and take a look at the people I meet along the way, I am forced to conclude that most countries (and, in fact, the world) are made up of individuals who live their lives according to what they imagine other people´s expectations of them are. And those who break this mold or pattern are going to find themselves going through a lot of pain. It´s only when we start experiencing that pain that we stop and reflect. When we go through a divorce. When we lose our job. When we get sick or lose someone close to us we care about. Only then do we call a halt.

But why? Why don´t we step back earlier – before it is too late – and ask ourselves some of the more fundamental questions? Why don´t we stop and notice what feels right and what feels wrong long before this? The brain is an amazing tool that helps us to live every single day. But the brain is also, to a great extent, a restraining force if there is no connection between the mind and the soul. It happens when you cannot sense deep inside, what feels right and what feels wrong. When we don´t trust our gut instinct, i.e. our intuition, then, all too often, we choose to make decisions based on what mental rationalization indicates is right. A rationalization usually colored by what we think those around us expect of us. Very often, these are not expectations which have been verified in any way, but which we presume exist, and so, taking them into consideration, we then start living by them.

WHAT MAKES YOU HAPPY?

We forget to pause occasionally and ask ourselves what would make us happy. We are always searching for something more, something better. We get divorced because we convince ourselves that this will make us happier, that the grass is greener on the other side. We change jobs, hoping that another job will be more satisfying, and stop us longing for something more. We constantly surround ourselves with other people in the hope that they – and not ourselves – will make us happy. We fill up our lives. We want more. We want something that we don´t have.

But basically, what it comes down to in the end is that we human beings, we individuals, are not really aware of what does, in fact, make us happy. For when I ask people, "What makes you happy?" people generally reply, "Well, of course, my wife and children, or my husband and children…" Those who are not married and are childless may say, "My dog, my cat, or even my goldfish." And this is true, of course. These things are some of the things that make us happy. But that is not the whole picture. They play a fundamental role in our lives, but they should not be the only things that make us happy.

Freedom is, to a great extent, one of the keys to being truly happy. For if we feel limited in some way restricted then we cannot feel happy. When we feel imprisoned, then we cannot be happy. When we feel that people are forcing us to do things that go against our beliefs, our very identity, then we cannot be happy either.

TAKING THINGS FOR GRANTED

The real problem is that we take an awful lot for granted. We take ourselves for granted, we take each other for granted, and we take our lives for granted. And when we take things for granted, we don´t stop. And when we don´t reflect on things, we don´t stop either. And if we don´t do this, we never find the answer to what will make us happy.

With this book, it is my aim to lead you to a new place. I want to help guide you from the unconscious to the conscious level. It is my fervent wish that, after having read my book, you will start living your life according to your own expectations, and that, in turn, will enable you to be more aware of what you have to offer others. Once you become more aware of your own qualities, become more aware of who *you* are, and what you have to offer both yourself and others, something quite unbelievable will happen. You will find that many of your dreams will come true. You will experience a level of success in your life, which you had never before dared to dream of or imagine.

IF YOU´RE GOING THROUGH A TOUGH TIME

Of course, there are circumstances in life that we cannot do anything about. We cannot change them. We can neither dream nor think our way out of them. BUT – you *can* decide what you want to have in your life, where you are headed, or would like to be, and what basic feelings you would like to feel in the future.

It is important for me to emphasize that I am not preaching any kind of miracle cure or trying to distort the truth in any way here. Not at all. I am fully aware that sometimes we humans find ourselves in situations during our lives that we simply cannot change. Situations that render us incapable of moving on, no matter how much we would like to. Circumstances that mean we are stuck where we are for awhile. People we suddenly lose or have to say goodbye to. And find ourselves stumbling around in the dark, despondent, where everything feels hopeless. We can learn to live with grief in our hearts. Grief doesn´t just disappear. It takes time. A long time. At times, we humans experience adversity and challenges and it takes time to understand what they mean. It may be difficult to pick ourselves up again. Pick ourselves up and look to the future. Believe in the good and believe that things surely will be alright.

Perhaps you find yourself in just such a place now. Perhaps you are hurting deep inside. Perhaps you are angry because you feel that every time you try, you fail. Every time you think that your dream is finally about to come true, you are disappointed.

This book cannot provide all the solutions. It is not a "*quick fix*" – not a "one size fits all" solution – to any problem or challenge life may throw at you. It does, however, offer some insight into a mindset that I have benefitted greatly from in my life. And I have seen how others have been helped and guided by this mindset, too.

Wherever we are in our lives, as a rule, new paths and fresh approaches do open new doors. And that is what I hope you will discover. That you will perhaps open a new door that will allow you to see the world from a whole new perspective.

I hope you will enjoy reading "The Life Bridge".

Ulrik

CHAPTER 2

WHAT ARE YOUR DREAMS?

"If you really want to dream,
be fully awake."

Paulo Coelho

YES! WHAT YOU DREAM OF CAN COME TRUE.

Is it really possible to attract most of your dreams?

I am convinced that it really is possible. I believe that it is only our own beliefs, our own mind, our own thoughts that limit our hopes and aspirations.

So does that mean that we can fly if we want to? No, of course not. Some scientific elements create limitations. But, basically, you are the one who sets your own limits with regard to what you wish for and dream of, and what you wish to attract in your dreams.

The majority of people I meet have no doubt whatsoever about all the things they do *not* dream of. All those things we don't want: I don't want to get sick. I don't want to lose my job. I don't want to get divorced. I don't want to die young. The word "don't" is repeated over and over, and we are certainly very aware of all the things we don't want.

Often, when I give a person a piece of paper and ask them to write down all the things they don't want in their lives, versus all the things they do – sure enough, the "don't" list often turns out to be much longer than the list of dreams.

A PROBLEM-FREE EXISTENCE

For many people the term "dream" is a very abstract one. Most of us are simply not aware of what we actually dream about.

Dreaming doesn't only have to be about things like climbing Mount Everest! It could just as easily be about a comfortable daily existence. Days filled with more happy moments than bumps along the way.

Does this sound familiar? When you arrive at someplace you have to be, which has a limited amount of parking spaces, you can be sure that there won't be any left for you when you get there.

Let me tell you something – the only thing standing in your way is how you look at it the situation. Let me give you an example.

I have a lunch with one of my old bosses – a nice guy - a couple of times a year. We meet up at the same cozy restaurant every year. There are eight parking places outside this restaurant. The thing is, this is an extremely popular little place and virtually everyone in Denmark eats lunch at the same time. So, of course, this means that everyone arrives at the same place at the same time. So you don't have to be a mathematical genius to work out that with 8 parking spaces and maybe 50 guests who all bring their own cars, these spaces disappear pretty quickly around lunch time.

Despite that, I always get a space right out in front. My dear old boss is almost always standing outside waiting for me, watching me, get a parking space right outside the door, not just once but every single time – while he is forced to park almost a quarter of a mile away. Every time I get out of the car his reaction is the same: "SO HOW COME *YOU* CAN GET A PARKING SPOT WHEN NONE OF THE REST OF US CAN?"

My answer is always the same: "My dear friend, just ask for help and you'll get a parking space."

"You can make simply make up your mind that *of course* there will be a space, and you will soon begin to notice that never again will you have a problem getting a parking space." It may sound weird to you, but believe me – it works.

Let me give you another example.

You have to do something very important. Something you have really been looking forward to for a long time, and suddenly the thought occurs to you, "I hope I don't get sick." Here comes the problem. You can't get that thought out of your mind. You keep on thinking, "I hope I don't get sick." – so what happens next? You get SICK.

I am rarely sick for I only think about being well. I made a decision a long time ago that I wanted to be well instead of sick, and so I avoid being sick almost all of the time.

I know that these examples are very simple, everyday examples, but for me, they illustrate very effectively that what you think, is what you'll attract. You can decide whether or not there will be a parking space. You can decide whether or not you will make the plane or train in time. You can decide whether your car or another car will get that parking spot. You can decide whether or not to be sick. And so on, and so on. For the thoughts you have, attract what you want - and the universe is listening to you and helping you on your way.

ABOUT ATTRACTING DREAMS

One of the primary reasons that I have succeeded in making almost all of my dreams come true is that I have *believed* that they would in one way or another. Earlier on, I did this subconsciously. As time passed – during the last 2-3 years – while I have been working intensively on developing my own consciousness, I have realized that almost every single time I have had a new dream, I have had faith that I would succeed.

I have not doubted it for a second. And believing totally in what we dream of is one of the main elements in being able to attract our dreams. The moment you allow doubt to creep in, you dissipate the focus and energy that is required to attract the dream. On the other hand, if we believe wholeheartedly that this is the right dream for me, and direct all our energy towards it, then we stand a greater chance of attracting it.

You are probably sitting there thinking, "Hmmm, I don't think in terms of dreams. I have no idea what I dream of, so how am I going to get started on this dreaming business?"

THE DIFFERENCE BETWEEN A GOAL AND A DREAM

You might also be thinking, "What is the difference between setting a goal and having a dream?"

Most goal-oriented types set themselves a positive goal to achieve. Right away, they draw up a plan of how to achieve this goal. Once they have made this plan, which may take a considerable amount of time, they also set up what are often referred to as "milestones". These help them to stick to the plan all the way through, and achieve the success criteria in gradual steps, before actually reaching the final goal.

But let us imagine that you pause for a moment and identify one of the goals you have reached - one of the dreams you have perhaps fulfilled – and reflect on the original plan you made, compared to the plan which reality forced upon you. The path you had to follow in real life. How alike were they really?

When I ask other people this question – whether in business or privately– most people come up with the same answer: Those plans did not resemble each other very much at all – in fact, perhaps not at all.

Steve Jobs once held a keynote speech in which he spoke about 'Connecting the Dots'. Simply put, "Connecting the Dots" stated that when we dream and set goals for ourselves, it is fine to identify the elements which should be included in these dreams, or identify the goal we wish to achieve. However, we cannot control the route taken to realize these dreams.

I can hear that perhaps you are still thinking, "OK, so why are we talking about dreams rather than goals? Why don't we talk about company dreams instead of company strategies?"

For me, I envisage a goal as a thought process, but a dream as a feeling.

And once we can feel something at an emotional level, then we are also able to identify more closely with it. And when we can identify with it as the person and individual we are, then we are in a much better position to create the focus that is needed and maintain the energy level we require to attract that dream.

HOW DO YOU ATTRACT A DREAM?

Let me give you an example.

When I was about 13 years old, Olympus brought out a new camera with a display screen and zoom lens. This was simply the coolest camera ever. It cost almost $500 which was completely out of my price range at that time. I had a paper round, delivering newspapers. Twice a week no less. I think I earned around $50 a month doing this. In other words, it was not going to be anytime in the near future that I was going to get my dream camera.

Nevertheless, every week I dropped by the photographer's store. They were sympathetic, even though they were probably getting slightly fed up of me. I got ahold of the brochure which I read over and over every single day. I read it so many times, in fact, that after a month I had to go back and get a new one, as it was falling to bits. But, doggedly, I continued… and continued. In my mind's eye, I visualized the pictures I would take. How I would feel standing there with that camera, how I would feel taking pictures with that camera. I could physically feel the emotions it stirred in me – the dream of owning that camera for myself. And I carried on determinedly, wanting that camera, attracting it, reading about it, and checking it out at the photographer's.

Then I took a trip to London with my parents. To make a long story short, unfortunately, my mother had her handbag stolen. But that bag contained some of my things. And when the insurance company calculated the damages to be awarded, it turned out that the total value of the articles I had lost in this incident totaled $500. And it was this $500 I used to go down to the photographer's store and purchase the camera I had dreamed of. That was the first time that one of my biggest dreams came true.

BE SPECIFIC ABOUT WHAT YOU WISH FOR

The important point about this story is that you have to be specific about exactly how you want to attract your dream. Because if you are not specific about how you will attract that dream and the elements you'd like included, then you will not be in any position to influence how that dream you're attracting turns out.

I once had a client who told me that she wanted $35,000. This would ease her tight financial situation considerably. So she visualized this $35,000 over and over again. Sure enough she got this amount 3 months later. The only problem was that this $35,000 was the amount of redundancy pay that accompanied her pink slip.

She had not yet found the answer as to why this had happened until I talked to her and asked, "But did you specify exactly where this money should come from?" She hadn't. I explained to her how everything is interconnected, that what we think is what we attract. When we are not *specific* about which elements we want to have included in our dream, then we can't expect to have any influence over the precise form in which it arrives.

And by "*specific*", I mean that you must give some thought to what the underlying higher purpose of your dream is.

Why exactly do I dream of running a marathon in New York? Why do I dream about travelling around the world? If I dream about going off traveling, where would I like to go? Which countries? What time of year? Why those places in particular?

BEING SPECIFIC ALSO MEANS MAKING A CONSCIOUS CHOICE

When we are more specific, then we also become more aware of the elements that are required to attract our dream. We need to be able to visualize the dream. Perhaps begin by reading about the dream or the precise feeling that dream gives you. For example, the feeling or concept of freedom forms the basis of all of my dreams.

We must also remember, however, that we do have a day-to-day existence. A here and now. And an awful lot of people forget to live in the present once they begin to dream.

This is what "The Life Bridge" is all about. The balance between those dreams and the here and now. The balance between the present and the future. The balance between dreaming big, while being grateful for what you have today.

For me, "The Life Bridge" has been a life-changing model that explains why I have been successful in most of my endeavors in life.

It is also one of the reasons why I basically wake up happy each and every morning, and go to bed content at night.

For it is a question of becoming aware of all the things we love and value. Of being grateful for the lives we are living today. Yet, at the same time, it is also just as much about becoming more consciously aware of the kind of future life you would like to have one day.

What kind of things do I want to fill my life with?

What kind of life do I want to lead?

What dreams do I want to fulfill?

What do I want to do with my life, and how do I get the very most out of it?

How do I live my life to its full potential?

What links these two elements together- the "here and now" and the dream – is energy. And it is this energy I am referring to when I talk about a "higher purpose" in this book, a universal power, something divine. It is also this energy I am referring to when I talk about attraction.

There are thus only two elements that we need to be aware of: an awareness of everything that I love in my life today, here and now, and an awareness of what I would like to happen tomorrow. In other words, my dreams. Two elements!

HAVE FAITH AND REMAIN HUMBLE. YOU CANNOT CONTROL TIME.

Have faith that, in time, you will be granted the things that you desire. But remember to be patient. Unshakeable faith combined with patience is what is needed. Patience because things take time, and according to Einstein, the aspect of time is merely an illusion. But time is what is required in order for the energy to collect around the two elements of "The Life Bridge". Having faith means more than simply being patient. Faith is just as much a question of believing in your dream, of believing that what you think is what you will attract. Do you believe that "The sky is not the limit, the mind is"? If you begin to doubt your faith and your dream, then you will create your own limitations, limit your own energy. That means that you yourself will subconsciously block the energy that is needed, and will not then be able to attract your dreams.

If we do not grant time the respect it is due, then we do not show respect for the elements that we want to be included in our dream either, or for the things we should be grateful for in our lives here and now.

The result of this is that right away this energy will begin to dissipate and the two balance points (Heart/Dream) will move farther away from each other. And this means that your dreams and the possibility of achieving them fade and recede into the distant future.

We must become more aware of all the things we should be truly grateful for, and remain humble about the life we have now. At the same time, we need to define our dreams more clearly, and respect the fact that time is not something we can control.

When we reach this stage – and only when we reach this exact point – can our dreams be fulfilled.

CHAPTER 3

HOW DO YOU PRIORITIZE? MORE ABOUT UNCONSCIOUS AND CONSCIOUS CHOICES

"Only dead fish go with the flow."

DO YOU GIVE A LOT OF THOUGHT TO WHAT YOU DO AND DON´T CHOOSE IN LIFE?

Throughout life, we are presented with a huge number of choices.

It is important to be aware of why you make the choices you do. In my opinion, learning to prioritize is a combination of being able to narrow down what is important to you, and then being make decisions based on that. This does not necessarily mean that you should make selfish choices, but simply that you are aware of what your preferences are.

Learning to prioritize is not an easy task, by any means. There are advantages and disadvantages in every choice. It can made even more difficult, however, if you lack focus and choose instead to take the easy way out by going along with what others expect you to achieve, instead of making your own choices. The journey towards narrowing down and then making your own choices requires a great deal of inner reflection, and you will need to probe your memory for the moments and actions that have made you really happy in the past. Once you begin to explore the feeling of happiness those moments brought you, then you are starting to learn how to choose based on conscious wishes instead of fear. In other words, you are making a choice based on what you believe will make you happier, rather than choosing the least risky option, the one that will make you least unhappy, or will present the least number of problems.

In addition to inner reflection, another key element in the prioritization process is that of keeping things simple. Try not to let yourself be influenced by practical issues, because this will only make things far more complicated. Start your prioritization process with the mindset that "anything is possible", and "there are no obstacles or limitations" in your path. This will allow you to think and react more creatively in achieving your priorities. You should also keep in mind that timing has a role to play in this equation, , too, and that the timing of your priorities can have a great impact on your life. The important thing here is to exclude any kind of restriction, and just feel and write down your dreams.

By focusing on the actual emotion the dream creates, you will find that the range of opportunities expands the more you begin to realize the degree to which various actions/situations/circumstances match your priorities in life.

ARE YOU LIVING THE LIFE YOU DREAMED OF?

Perhaps deep inside you feel that you are really not living the life you would like to live? Realizing and admitting that you are not living your ideal life can be quite hard. Once you have reached that conclusion, you have to admit that it hurts – REALLY hurts.

I think a lot of people can put their hands up to that, and when I began to realize that many things in my life did not match what was truly important to me, it hurt a lot, too. A LOT. I realized that the path I thought my life was going to follow was not really a path at all. It was more of a dead-end – a precipice even. That made me begin to question everything about my life.

The biggest question was WHO AM I?, What do I want to do with my life? What makes me happy? What energizes me? – and most importantly of all, What is the meaning of my life?

While searching for answers to these basic questions, I also gained some insight into decisions I had made earlier. Decisions, which at first glance, I was sure I had made based on other people´s expectations, but gradually began to realize were, in fact, my *own* expectations projected onto those around me. That is, expectations that had never been put into words or indicated in any way. Expectations that *I* had created internally, not ones that came from the outside world. Expectations I had of myself that were designed to convince the outside world that I had my life under control, and that I was a success.

During the many hours I spend talking to other people, I can see clearly that they do the same thing. I am convinced that the pattern I followed is by no means unique. I can see that many of the people I work with every day act according to the expectations they think others have of them. They are not even aware they are doing it, so therefore they spend a vast number of resources analyzing their way through life, convincing themselves that that they have figured out what those around them expect of them, but forgetting themselves in the process. They do themselves a lot of harm, both in the present and in the future.

The break-through that changed my life – that helped me learn to love myself – was to ask myself a simple question when I woke up every day: "Ulrik, what do you expect of yourself today and what can you offer those around you?"

Before this, my thought went something like: "Ulrik, I wonder what the world expects of me today – and can I live up to those expectations?"

Ask yourself the following question: "Who is the most important person in your life?" Your first thought will most likely be those closest to you.

But remember: YOU are the most important person in your life. If you don´t do this and react likewise, then in the long run, you will mean very much to others either. So take control of your life and decisions. Don´t live your life according to expectations you presume others have of you, instead create your own expectations and live up to them.

MAKE A LIST OF YOUR PRIORITIES

For me, priorities are primarily about making active choices, and even more importantly, actively opting out where necessary. In other words, making an active choice as to what you want out of life, rather than just existing on autopilot – or doing what everybody else is doing. If you want to gain an understanding of what it is YOU really want, then you need to know what your priorities are.

Let me set you a little challenge. Take two pieces of paper. Write down all the things you would like to have in your life on one – and all the things you don't want to have in your life, on the other. Compare these two lists and think about what your current life looks like. What does it contain? What are the majority of points? Negative or positive? Do your current life and your priorities match what you dream of deep inside?

Let's pursue this a little further. Give a little more thought to the things you dream about.

Why, for example, would you like to have a good, well-paid job? My guess would be because you would like to be recognized for the contribution you can make to your field, while learning more, feeling that you fit in, and earning a good salary to boot.

This kind of thought process this can help sharpen your prioritizing skills. In this case, it might mean looking for a new job, where you will achieve greater recognition for your efforts. Remember that your thoughts play a significant role here. So if you have a positive mindset when working with your feelings, everything will come easier to you, because you are mentally prepared for it. By paying attention to your feelings and being aware of your behavior when you prioritize, you can go far, and can help yourself to achieve a better quality of life.

Connecting with our values and emotions, reflecting upon our current life and comparing all of these to each other, can have a significant impact. Knowing your own personal values and reacting according to them, can produce positive results in terms of increased levels of commitment, increased efficiency and a strong performance, as well as deep sense of enjoyment. In terms of your daily life, behaving according to your own values is a strength. Reflecting on which tasks and personal relationships promote your values can help set you on the right course, and also increase your overall feeling of happiness and self-development. Conversely, not remaining true to your own core values can be very damaging and can lead to such things as low levels of involvement, and, in the worst-case case scenario, stress and depression. This happens mainly (and usually without being consciously aware of it) because you are doing things that do not relate in any way whatsoever to your goals (in life), or are even working against them.

Taking a broader perspective, it's all about having the ability to make conscious choices in daily life in relation to the things that fill you with energy and the goals that you want to pursue.

THE IDENTITY LEADERSHIP MODEL

I have developed a model that will help you to delve deeper into your self-awareness.

"The Identity Leadership Model" is a model to promote inner-reflection, which can be used to evaluate yourself in the most significant areas of your life, such as career, family, hobbies, friends, etc. Once you realize where you are in each of these areas, your future immediately becomes clearer. In each life-space mentioned, evaluate where you are in three areas–your heart, your energy and your dreams. By combining the various tools for inner-reflection that are provided, you will be able to make an honest assessment of these different areas, using three specific parameters:

On a scale from 0 to10, how would you rate yourself?	❤	🔋	☁	ILS Potential
Being with *myself*				100%
Being with my *closest family*				100%
Being with my *children*				100%
Being with my *friends*				100%
Being at *work*				100%

HEART, ENERGY AND DREAMS

The Heart represents the authentic self. That is, the degree to which you can "be yourself" in various situations. Are you, in fact, able to just be yourself, or do you try to adapt to other's expectations of you? Perhaps you think that you always act the same, but once you start to pay attention, you will notice that this is not the case. You will notice that sometimes our behavior varies with the situation and thus so, too, do our opportunities to be our authentic selves. This applies both horizontally and vertically in the model. For the degree to which we feel able to be ourselves, for example, may depend on which member of the family or friend we are with. Just as we may also act very differently with friends, compared to when we are together with our respective spouse/ or relationship partner - or when we are alone.

The Cloud represents your dreams. Your conscious direction. Where you want to go. It is also equally about how you can see whether you are progressing or developing. So if it is about your friends, for instance, the question is: What do you get out of being together with these individuals? Are they people you get together with regularly, and do you have a good time when you are together – yet don´t really care one way or the other whether you see them or not? Are you left with a feeling of emptiness after each time you´re together? An emptiness that in reality stems from the fact that this person/these people don´t have anything to offer you? The opposite of this is when you can see some growth. When you can feel that your relationship is progressing. Perhaps you don´t know where it is leading, but that is not so important. The important thing is that we are developing together, moving forward together in the direction in which we wish to go. This is true for everything in life. It is a fact that the world is constantly changing, and therefore, we must accept that we need to keep up and be more consciously aware of the direction in which we are moving.

The Battery represents energy, of course. That is, the question of what your energy level is like in different situations. Are you full of energy or drained of energy?

Obviously, if you have small children who require all your energy and focus, then it can be difficult to summon up energy in that situation. I am talking more about being conscious of the energy in people and situations. Having an awareness of energy will help you understand whether or not you are using your resources correctly. Whether you are in the right relationship. Or whether you have friends who drain you for energy more than they fill you up. Or whether you are actually ruining your own life because your job is sucking all the positive energy out of you.

Let me give you an example. I had a mentoring session with a CEO who basically was looking for the answer to the question: "Shall I retire or not?"

He was 60 years old and didn´t really feel ready to be put out to pasture just yet. During the many months of dialogue we had in the course of these mentoring sessions, we had worked on gaining more insight on and defining the most important elements in his business life, as well as his private life. We had created an overview of his dreams and all the things that were important to him. Despite all this, making this decision was proving to be a big challenge for him.

A few days after I had finished my work on the ILS model, my client arrived for yet another mentoring session, where I introduced him to the model. I explained the thinking behind it, and how we were going to work with it. He chose to carry out an evaluation on himself, his wife, his mother, his son, his friends and work. Point for point, we examined his heart, energy and dreams and came to this result.

On a scale from 0 to 10, how would you rate yourself?				ILS Potential
Being with *myself*	7	8	7	61%
Being with my *closest family*	10	9	9	19%
Being with my *children*	10	9	6	46%
Being with my *friends*	9	9	8	35%
Being at *work*	5	4	6	88%

When he was finished he said, "Could I just call my wife?"

He called his wife and his first words were, "Hi darling, I´ve made the decision. I´m stopping work at the end of the year." That was the end of the conversation.

I asked what had made him make that decision and he answered, "When I had finished my ILS model, I reached the conclusion that everything I had chosen to evaluate on my ILS was positive. I felt authentic in all areas. I feel that I can clearly see the way ahead, and receive positive energy from all areas EXCEPT my work. It's a struggle day and night. It is getting harder and harder for me to be the person I really am. I find it difficult to relate to the direction we are moving in – I can't see myself there in 5 years time – and worst of all, all of this is having a negative effect on my energy levels. All at once it hit me, that all the other parameters would improve even more the day I stop, so the time has come to retire."

It was my last session with that client, but that was fine because he had found the answer to what would really make him happy.

WHAT DO *HEART, ENERGY AND DREAMS* MEAN TO YOU?

It can actually be quite difficult to answer some perfectly simple questions. "What makes me happy?", or "What energizes me?", "What do I dream of?"

In my experience, most people name things which contribute to their basic support structure. By this, I mean that people refer to those they care about, or things that provide them with a feeling of security and fulfill their physical needs, as well as things that help people fulfill their own potential such as creativity, morality, freedom, etc.

In the context of Maslow's "Hierarchy of Needs", these appear to be quite basic needs. Nevertheless, it is difficult for most people to put their finger on exactly what makes them happy, what gives them energy, and what they dream of. They are simply not able to dig deep and discover just what their passion in life might be.

By applying this insight to something like the number of unmotivated employees in the world, one could claim that the lack of motivation or commitment is due to the fact that many people only show up at work to fulfill their basic needs (income, security, etc.) and are not actively seeking to fulfill any "higher purpose" but, if they did, it would mean we'd end up with a 100% committed workforce, who cared passionately about what they were doing!

Similarly, there are a vast number of young people who choose a college education that deep down isn't really what they'd like to pursue. They choose their education with their head, instead of following their gut feeling about what they'd really like to do. We may face the same challenges in our private life, too. We may choose to stay together with our partner partly for rational reasons; not always listening to what our heart is really telling us.

My point is that if you start by prioritizing according to what makes you happy and what you feel you can contribute, then you will end up much happier in life. Once you have got a feel for which elements are important to you, you will realize that you have often prioritized wrongly in the past.

Prioritizing according to what makes you happy, can be the forerunner to achieving a deeper insight into yourself and what makes you tick. An increased sense of inner awareness, which is a "must" on your route to finding your dreams – and fulfilling those dreams.

CHAPTER 4

INSIGHT PROVIDES PERSPECTIVE

"If you find a path with no obstacles it probably doesn't lead anywhere."

Frank A. Clark

IT IS TIME FOR YOU TO LOOK INWARDS – A LITTLE MORE DEEPLY

I could also have called this chapter "Moving from the unconscious to the conscious". That is, in fact, what all of this book is all about. About making you more aware of who you are. More aware of your dreams. More aware of the life you are leading right now. Aware of your choices and what you don´t choose. It is, in fact, about bringing about a fundamental change from you – perhaps – current state of unconsciousness.

Being unconscious means, among other things, that you are also not aware of all the wonderful and positive things that are most certainly a part of your life.

I´m willing to bet that taking things for granted, instead of being grateful and humble, has a direct and powerful influence on things such as divorce statistics. We are never quite satisfied. We want something more, something else.

The same thing applies when we forget to dream. We are running on a never-ending treadmill, like hamsters on a wheel, without knowing why. We may think we know why, but never stop to question it, and are all too often driven by other´s expectations. Sometimes we find ourselves wondering how we got to where we are in our lives. We have forgotten why it was so important.

For example, when we first meet someone new, we are curious because we don´t have all the answers about who they are, so we start exploring, probing every corner to find out just who this person is. In romantic relationships, we try to find out how this person ticks, who they are mentally, emotionally and physically, and whether this person is someone we can identify with. But as time goes by, the energy we invest in this dissipates. We forget to be curious.

It's a question of remaining conscious of things – in all aspects of life. Be conscious about how you use your time. Who you spend it with? Be conscious of why you go to work in the mornings, why you live where you do, where you go, why you live as you do. You should ask yourself these questions. You should give yourself the gift of moving from a state of unconsciousness in your current life to a state of being fully aware of everything it contains. For only once you do this, will you be in a position to put into words what it is you want to change. In other words, you will then be able to say your dreams out loud, and begin to identify how you will fulfill those dreams. How you should structure and plan your life so those dreams can come true.

ARE YOU GRATEFUL FOR WHAT YOU HAVE – OR DO YOU TAKE IT ALL FOR GRANTED?

Let me use relationships as an example. We all know that, as time goes by and we allow things to fall into an everyday routine, habits and roles become entrenched. Perhaps we begin to take each other for granted. Just as we begin to take ourselves for granted, our health for granted. In fact, we often take our whole life for granted, our career for granted, our parents for granted, our siblings for granted. We take our freedom for granted as well. The list is incredibly long, and all too often we forget that the very things we take for granted are those which some other person dreams of having, but because those things are there all the time, we often forget to appreciate them.

But the fact is that the world is constantly changing. We used to say that the only sure thing in life was death. Today, we must face the fact that there are now two things that are certain in life. The first is still that we are going to die, but the next is that the world is constantly changing, and will continue to do so. What this means is that, consciously or unconsciously, we people are also constantly changing. But we forget this simple fact. We forget that we, as people, evolve. And, along the way, we forget to be grateful. We focus only on the treadmill, as we keep on running – in a cycle that bores and frustrates us.

Many people have no answers when they are asked what they have to be grateful for and what they take for granted. Not right off the top of their heads at any rate. But the answers are there deep inside us. We are the world's largest encyclopedia when it comes to the subject of us! We just don't always realize it, and that's a shame. For if we can only learn to understand ourselves better, if we become better at paying homage to the life we have, while making more conscious and active choices about what we want to do and not do – then we will be getting closer to living a life that holds some meaning for us. An authentic life. A life you could only dream of before.

That is precisely why gaining insight about yourself is so important. Because insight provides you with perspective. The perspective that helps you understand who and what should be in your life. So therefore: Decide what you want to have in your life. Decide what you as a family, as a couple, as friends want to have in your life. Build your dream around this. Attract it using the energy you possess. See and feel what a huge difference it makes.

The Dalai Lama once said: "If you want to learn something new, then stop talking and start listening more." The ability to listen to yourself and your inner voice is the route to finding the answers you seek.

PERHAPS YOU ARE AFRAID OF THE SILENCE THAT LIES IN JUST LISTENING?

It is by no means easy to look inwards. To seek change. To search for a new meaning in life. It takes courage. The big changes in life take even more courage and energy than normal, especially if they are the kind of changes that require you to stop and re-evaluate every aspect of your life.

When you are faced with changes in your life, it's only natural to be afraid – be it consciously or unconsciously. Fear begins to creep in. The fear of what lies in wait. The fear of making mistakes. Whether it be changes in your working life, romantic relationship or anything else in life, they all lead to the unknown. So it is only natural that we feel afraid and would really prefer to avoid making any changes at all. Would prefer to remain on safe ground. To stay where we are – even if the place we are in doesn't really make us very happy.

Perhaps initially, what tempts us to resist change and stops us wanting to move on, is our fear of facing up to the truth – being afraid of what this might say about the life we are living now. But try and embrace change and development. Don't close your eyes and refuse to look at opportunities that might help you develop yourself. Instead, listen to what your heart and head tell you. Your heart knows what is best for you and your heart – well, what can I say – it always has your best interests at heart!

The more we suppress our wishes, the more we will begin to sense that something is wrong – that something is missing. That we are not completely satisfied. We cannot feel who we really are, or have forgotten who we are. We feel only a sense of dissatisfaction.

If that is how you feel, then I urge you to take a look at your current life, the choices you have made and those you haven´t. I challenge you to take responsibility for your life. For by taking responsibility, you will be able to create the life you dream of. And it will give you an enormous sense of freedom.

DO YOU KNOW YOUR OWN BEHAVIORAL PATTERNS?

I touch on this subject many times throughout this book. Self-knowledge provides you with a better perspective. Or expressed in another way: Once you understand your own behavioral patterns, you will be ready and able to open yourself up to a new reality. A reality in which you live in greater harmony with your soul, your soul´s calling and your innermost dreams.

Reflecting on our own behavior gives us the benefit of discovering why we react as we do (which we do) in different situations.

We can distinguish between two different types of behavior: Innate behavior and learned behavior. Innate behavior is a person´s natural behavior, how we act towards others when we feel safe and relaxed. Learned behavior reflects the changes in personality and behavior we feel we need to make in order to fit in, in a given situation.

Knowing ourselves better, possessing self-knowledge, allows us to distinguish between these two types of behavior and to override our learned behavior. If, however, we are unable able to distinguish between these two types of behavior, a prolonged period of learned behavior can lead to negative consequences such as stress or depression. (Reference from Ensize)

THE PATH TO THE AUTHENTIC SELF IS VIA SELF-KNOWLEDGE

Generally, self-knowledge is closely linked to authenticity or the ability to be true to ourselves.

Being authentic means that we are aware of what we feel and how we think. Thus, we are able to react in a manner that makes it clear what we feel, in a manner that is in harmony with our heart and soul. We can tell if our behavior is authentic by thinking about how our personality (character traits) changes depending on the surroundings we find ourselves in. And then identifying which of these personalities (character traits) we feel most comfortable with.

Even though it is not necessarily a bad thing to adapt your personality to the situation, it is extremely important that we are clear about which traits we are overriding, which ones we have chosen, and how this feels. One example could be about the issue of child-rearing versus your working life. Are we the same person at home and at work? It is quite natural to change your personality in this set up, but it shouldn´t mean limiting ourselves in some way, otherwise we will end up feeling out of step with our authentic self.

Self-knowledge also means being aware of one´s own priorities, dreams and ambitions. I have met many people who have expressed a feeling of being stuck, or of not seeing the point in continuing in the direction they are headed. They have found it difficult to define their real priorities and have been unable to find something to be passionate about in their lives.

While not everyone lacks direction in their life, it is important to remind ourselves just what our priorities and dreams really are, as they influence our behavior. Being able to prioritize and dream also helps us foster clear intentions, and that helps us to communicate what we want to achieve to the outside world.

CHAPTER 5

YOU HAVE A CHOICE. NOW.

"Each morning
we are born again.
What we do today is
what matters most."

Buddha

IT IS, IN FACT, ALL UP TO YOU....AND ONLY YOU.

It is you, and *only* you, who decide what kind of life you will live. What you will feel, how you will act or react. You can actively change the circumstances of your life. You, and only YOU, can uproot yourself and move forward.

Once you begin to create an inner awareness about what you really dream of, you also set in motion an inner process. A process that, hopefully, will also express itself on the outside. But this can only happen if you choose to change. If you choose to follow YOUR wishes and dreams. If you choose to listen to yourself and the calling that comes from your soul.

One of my favorite questions that I put to most people is: "Do you think that we attract the things we think about? The thoughts and feelings we fill our minds with, the thoughts and feelings that fill our souls, is that what we'll also get in our lives? If we think big, then we'll get big, but if we think small, then that's what we'll get, if we think negative, we'll get a negative life and if we think positive, we'll get a positive life. Is that how it works?"

Most people answer yes. BUT only the very few live out their dreams. Most choose not to listen. To listen to the most important voice in their lives. Their own. You could say that they DISQUALIFY themselves in a sense.

Perhaps you can identify with this and are in a similar situation yourself at the moment, where you feel you have hit a dead-end? Where there is no light at the end of the tunnel, and you are telling yourself that I am probably convinced that you have brought it on yourself. At least, I can imagine that you might feel that my assertion is a load of garbage – intended just to provoke you.

I have spoken to over 500 different people about this very subject, so naturally, I have met many people who DIDN´T believe for one single minute that what they thought was what they attracted.

I am no guru and I certainly don´t have all the answers in life. But I can only say that those people who originally said that they didn´t believe it, without a single exception, eventually reached the conclusion that they themselves had brought their own probems upon themselves. Everyone I have spoken to has also realized that when we find ourselves in situations that REALLY hurt- where there seems to be no way out, and everything seems to be against us – these are the times in our lives that teach us the most. Once we get through these bad spells and come out on the other side, we also understand, if we give it some thought, why we had to go through such a tough experience.

It may well be that you feel that this doesn´t make any sense, and that what you´d really like to do is throw this book across the room, and, of course, that´s up to you, and OK if you do! But do yourselves a favor and pick it up again at some later date and you will discover brand new facets of yourself – and of the book as well probably.

DO YOU CHOOSE – OR REJECT FREEDOM IN YOUR LIFE RIGHT NOW?

I will mention this more than once in the course of this book. It´s interesting to note that if you ask people what they dream about, most people say things like winning the lottery, giving up work, traveling around the world or something similar.

For years, I´ve been getting the same answer, and for years I´ve been thinking about what people all over the world basically dream about, and I have reached the conclusion that this is what it is: Freedom.

Freedom is the ultimate element that overshadows everything else, that is the thing we all seek. The problem is that we just don´t realize it. But freedom is a basic feeling that everyone, throughout the generations, from the time of slavery through evolution until today, has longed for and needed.

No matter what your personal definition of freedom is, ask yourself whether you feel that sense of freedom now? Within yourself, in your relationship as part of a couple, in your working life? If the answer is no, then I would encourage you to read further. Because you CAN achieve freedom – not only the feeling of freedom, but actual freedom. And it WILL change your level of well-being, your level of happiness, your life. I promise you that. But to achieve this, you must first take a couple of steps. And the first step is TO CHOOSE: To actively choose to welcome that process into your life. You have to understand that in order to make your dreams come true, you have to make an effort to change. First, you must identify your dreams. Put them into words. Pay attention to your feelings. What are you REALLY dreaming of?

We mortals forget sometimes to let ourselves dream. Or else, we ´don´t actually know *how* to dream. Or we think that that winning a million in the lottery is our big dream. In my view, this is a big mistake.

Those who start dreaming and really explore their dreams in depth – really analyze their dreams – are far more likely to have them fulfilled. They will experience that what we dream is what we attract. What we dream of *can* be fulfilled.

All that is left is to ask: Do you want to make that choice? YOUR choice? The choice that means that- when you begin to look inwards – you will learn exactly what your dreams really are – and then good things will begin to happen to you. Will you join me on this journey? I hope so.

Let us take a look at our habits together in the next chapter. For if we are to shift our way of thinking, if we are to achieve anything greater than what we have now, then generally most of us have some bad habits that need to be broken first.

CHAPTER 6

ON HABITS – AND HOW WE BREAK THEM

"The secret to getting ahead is getting started."

Mark Twain

YOUR HABITS PLAY AN IMPORTANT ROLE IN DETERMINING WHETHER YOUR DREAMS WILL COME TRUE OR NOT

Habits can be a good thing in terms of our helping us to get things done. They can, for example, help you be disciplined when things sometimes get difficult. They are also important to our very existence, for without unconscious habits, we would need to engage our brain actively to, for example, breathe or walk or cycle. Nevertheless, it is equally true that habits can be harmful to the quality of our life if we do not give some thought to which ones we will let ourselves be controlled by.

It can actually be quite difficult to reflect on our own habits. It takes a good deal of self-refection and a high level of awareness, to pinpoint many of our habits as they are deeply ingrained in our whole way of thinking and being.

Healthy and positive mental habits, which support your own personal development, can help you learn to accept yourself as you are, and feel good about yourself, both of which will make you appreciate others more. Seeing yourself as "not good enough", reacting inappropriately when something unexpected happens, or avoiding certain situations are all habits which can prevent you from achieving your dreams.

Studies show that we humans think between 12.000-70.000 thoughts a day. Furthermore, most experts agree that over 80% of these thoughts are ones that are repeated each day. (Davis 2013). Thus, we can say that it is extremely important to identify exactly which ones get repeated. Habits repeat themselves according to the state our brain is in. So if we have a positive outlook on life, our brain will be influenced by that, and make it easier for us to repeat the positive thoughts.

What can you do if there is room for a little improvement in your way of thinking? Create new thoughts! You can actively trick your mind into thinking positive by becoming consciously aware of what you are thinking of and turning your outlook on life into a positive one. Being surrounded by positive people is also one way to give you a positive boost. Once you have assimilated these positive thoughts into your brain, then it's a question of letting "the snowball" roll down the slope, so it gets bigger and bigger.

66 DAYS IS ALL IT TAKES TO BREAK A HABIT

The average length of time it takes to change behavior/ or break a habit is around 66 days. Of course, it depends on the individual in question, and the situation they find themselves in. An example:

It took the participants in a previous study between 18 and 254 days to form a new habit. (Lally, Van Jaarsveld, Potts W., & Wardle, 2009)

Based on this study, we can see that it requires persistence and constant focused thought if we are to break our habits. Making a list of the habits you wish to break and pinning it up where you can see it every day is one helpful idea. You can also make a deal with friends, colleagues or your family, to form new habits either collectively or individually. What is most important to keep in mind is that we all have habits, and these can make an important contribution to our personal development and insight. By consciously thinking about the decisions which are made every day by our subconscious (habits), we can gain valuable insight into ourselves and change the undesirable subconscious decisions we make (habits). This paves the way for positive changes.

Experts have claimed that once we have identified our bad habits, we shouldn't try to break them, but instead replace them with better ones. This is because bad habits, in one way or another, are good for you. In some situations, they might help you cope with stress, yet could be harmful in other ways. Therefore, it can be beneficial to replace a bad habit with another that blocks the bad one.

Another important thing that experts recommend is cutting out all the small things that feed a bad habit. If you are self-employed and work from home, but end up doing more housework than work, perhaps it wouldn´t be a bad idea to find another place to work from. If your night on the town with friends always ends up in an orgy of junk food, why not prepare a more healthy alternative at home so you don´t need to buy anything. It´s also a great help if you can get other people to help you to break your bad habits. If both you and your friend would like to lose weight, why not prepare your meals and eat together. This also makes it harder to give up – and more fun to celebrate together when you reach your goal! Furthermore, it´s always a good idea to associate with friends and acquaintances that have the same good habits that you are striving for.

As we have discussed, one of the first steps towards changing and living out your dreams, is by examining your habits, the way you live, and what your daily existence is based on. Once you begin thinking about and identifying the habits you are not very happy about and are willing to change, this will make room for new habits and new energy that will support you in your process. The process in which you actively attract the future you desire for yourself.

CHAPTER 7

THE PLASTER EFFECT

"We were born to be real
not to be perfect."

Ralph Marston

DO YOU TEND TO NUMB THE PAIN?

Now that we have examined your habits in the previous chapter, we also need to take a closer look at a habit that many of us have. A habit which really doesn't do us any good at all. Why? Because it prevents us from actually seeing WHO we are, WHAT is good for us, and WHERE we should go from here in order to be happier and strengthen the connection between our heart, soul and abilities.

You can go through your whole life without ever really knowing who you are. Without listening to yourself, your dreams, your authentic self. A lot of people do just that. I call it numbing the pain. Or the *plaster effect*.

When we do not want to, do not dare to or are not yet ready to live a life that is completely authentic in every aspect, then we often fill it up with more of something. More noise. More things. More of something that perhaps makes us happy or satisfied for a short while. But it doesn't last. We put a plaster on the wound, instead of healing it. The wound represents the thing that needs our attention. The thing we need to examine more closely. If we cover the wound with a plaster, we close our eyes to the thing we really should have paid attention to and nursed back to health. I see it everywhere. People who stay in relationships that are not good for them. They would really like to get out of that unhealthy relationship, but don't dare. So they put a plaster on their feelings, even though they are hurting - they close their eyes and ignore the pain, an infection that will only spread over time, and fester and hurt even more.

For many couples, the plaster might be alcohol, cigarettes, infidelity – or renovating the house. A plaster is something that you make a grab for when you have feelings that become intolerable. You numb the pain, with something else to make it go away. But the question is. Does the pain go away? Or do you just prolong it, deadening it for a few moments

– knowing full well that the pain will return when the effects of the plaster have worn off?

THE DAY YOU LISTEN TO YOUR HEART, IS THE DAY YOU WILL NO LONGER NEED A PLASTER

I would urge you to take a look at yourself, your behavior and your behavioral patterns. Be totally honest with yourself. Do you numb the pain – instead of listening to yourself and taking responsibility for yourself and your happiness? Do you listen to the signals your body, heart and souls are sending you? I can promise you one thing. The day you begin to listen to those signals from your heart, and live authentically in harmony with them, is the first day you will truly feel happy and relaxed inside. It is so simple. So beautiful. And so true: The day you do that, is the day you will no longer need your plaster. Your plaster will no longer work, it will become immaterial. For in that instant, you will have healed yourself, your soul and your life.

You have a choice. And it is never too late to make the right choice, the one that is truly right for you. But perhaps you are feeling a bit confused? Perhaps you are not yet convinced about this business of your own conscious and subconscious actions? Perhaps, you are not yet aware of your own behavior?

CHAPTER 8

THE HEAD VS. THE HEART

"What you think you become,
what you feel you attract,
what you imagine you can create."

Buddha

FIRST OF ALL, A FEW WORD ABOUT SPIRITUALITY

This book is about growth, dreams and goals – about finding your own happiness. I am convinced, however, that we cannot shed any light on these things without looking at them through the eyes of spirituality.

For me, spirituality is about a deeper understanding of what it means to be a human being. Spirituality is a resource, a way of being that we can choose to use to great advantage in our personal development.

When you accept the insight that spirituality can provide us with, you will then be in a better position to help yourself and others to get as much out of your life and their lives as possible. To a large degree, it is all about understanding that we human beings form part of the universe and the universe, in turn, forms part of us.

The universal energy is what makes things happen, and it is this energy you need to attract and have faith in, in order to attract your dreams. It is the energy that forms part of your Life Bridge, which is the driving force that brings the life you wish to have in the future closer to the life you have now.

DOES YOUR HEAD OR YOUR HEART USUALLY WIN?

As I see it, the heart is a fortune-teller. The heart is connected to your soul. Your heart – your soul – knows best. Your heart knows you better than your head does. Your heart wants the very best for you. Your heart is loving. Your head is not necessarily so. Your head can fool you, confuse you, and frustrate you.

The toughest inner conflicts we humans get involved in, again and again throughout our lives, are the conflicts that arise between our heads and our hearts.

Most of us have been programmed from the day we were born to believe what the eye can see. Believe ONLY in listening to what our head and thoughts tell us. But our head fools us sometimes, and our head is not connected to the spiritual part of us. And if we want to connect with the authentic side of ourselves, then we MUST connect with our soul. And our head is not much use here.

But few of us have learned to see with our hearts, to listen to what our hearts and intuition are telling us. Believe in all those things you cannot necessarily see with the naked eye. Heart intelligence – the higher level of human intelligence – is about feeling with the heart and body, not just about using the head.

Initially, it may be very difficult for some of you to set aside your negative views on spirituality. So how do we open our minds?

We must allow ourselves to step outside our prejudices and current beliefs and dare to listen to our hearts and intuition and hear what they are saying.

Just because we have learned something because it is accepted as an "established social belief" or through stereotyping, that doesn´t make it true. Have you ever trusted your instincts and followed your intuition even when it made no sense? Even if everyone else thought you were barking up the wrong tree? But something in you told you it was right – it felt right. You knew it *was* the right way to go. And you actually felt as if you knew something no-one else did. Defying all logic, you went with your intuition instead.

YOUR HEART AND THE UNIVERSE TALK TO EACH OTHER

As I have said before, it takes a good deal of effort as well as courage, to achieve personal growth. In the beginning, it can also be difficult to hear what your heart and intuition are trying to tell you. But if you trust that your heart is linked to the universe, then perhaps you might dare to give your heart a chance? Have faith in what it is telling you, telling you forcefully – from a power that is greater than you.

This higher intelligence – the universe – will guide us if we allow it to. When we let go of logic, the head and the ego – and instead allow the universe and its higher intelligence to be heard – that, yes, *that* is when we suddenly connect to our true calling, our self, our innermost dreams.

Once we develop our spiritual intelligence (also known as heart intelligence), we will find greater peace and a greater meaning in our lives. Immediately. We will have moved closer to our Life Bridge. We will be closer to achieving complete balance.

In short: We become more at one with our authentic self and, thus, closer to our true dreams. Or put even more simply: When we LISTEN to our hearts, magic happens!

CHAPTER 9

LISTEN TO YOUR HEART

"Love is energy
and energy is everything."

HOW DO YOU LEARN TO LISTEN TO YOUR HEART?

"The most important things are invisible to the eye", said The Little Prince in the children´s book of the same name. And I can only reinforce this viewpoint again and again! YES. The most important things for you (and me) are not to be found in the outer world, but in a different place altogether. The most important things (when it comes to development on the higher spiritual plane) are stored in your heart – in your intuition.

Let me start by saying something. Learning to listen – just listen – to your heart and shut out all the other noise is, or can be, a lifelong process. It IS difficult. Especially in our western culture. For no-one has taught us how.

But that is no excuse. We must learn to connect to our heart´s messages if we are to reach the core of who we are, and what dreams we really carry inside us. Remember: It is only when we 1) learn to appreciate the here and now – and 2) really understand what our true dreams are – that we can make those dreams come true. And are able to achieve a perfect balance on our "Life Bridge".

Learning to listen to your heart takes time. If you are not used to "hearing" what it has to say, in the beginning, you will not receive any clear messages. You won´t be able to hear them for all the noise. I have mentioned this noise before. All those things you use to numb your pain. Other´s expectations. Your own habits. All this chatter interferes with your heart´s – your intuition´s –voice. Therefore, it is extremely important that you set aside some time to learn to listen to your inner messages, and have patience. Deep inside, you often know the answer to the big questions in your life. You just need to listen to the answer when it comes to you. Once you have practiced this a little, you will easily be able to feel what is right for you.

A LITTLE ABOUT THE HEART AND HEART MEDITATION

The heart plays a far greater role in the body than simply functioning as a pump.

The heart and our digestive system have a network of thousands of neurons that act as small "brain cells" in the body. These neurons have the ability to perceive things and are directly connected to the emotional part of the brain. All of this directly influence our brain. In addition, the brain may effect the whole organism through its electromagnetic field (which can be detected up to several feet away from the body) in a way which we do not fully understand today.

The link between the emotional brain and the "heart´s brain cells" is, as it turns out, the whole key to mastering the emotions. By learning to focus on the heart, e.g. by visualizing during meditation that we are drawing a gentle, white light into the heart with every intake of breath, we can have a positive effect on the emotional brain.

Meditating is not easy by any means. It requires the ability to focus deeply and be very patient, as it takes time to learn to let go of your constant stream of thoughts. Meditation is all about achieving a state of serenity in the moment, and letting your thoughts be just thoughts, your feelings just feelings, your fear just fear, and time just time. In other words, just enjoying the act of being – and letting go. Breathing techniques and an awareness of how you breathe is the key to mastering meditative skills and the meditative state. Therefore, this means that you need to focus 100% on your breathing, nothing else, and breathe from as far down in the stomach as you can.

There are several ways to get started on meditation. Some people download step-by-step meditation instructions from the internet, while others prefer to enjoy the company of other people in a meditation group. Staring out into space, going for a run, or letting go of your thoughts in some other way, can be just as much a form of meditation. Try to find the method that works best for you.

By allowing yourself 5 minutes of meditation in the morning, you can reduce the amount of the stress hormone, cortisol, in the body, and if you practice heart meditation before you go to bed, for example, your quality of sleep will improve.

It is important to understand that that the heart is a switchboard – with information and messages you should take seriously. You must learn to be observant and listen. To trust your intuition which is connected to your heart at a deep level.

Well then, so far so good. Now I have shared with you my thoughts about the heart. The heart which is really a tool for your intuition. I will mention the idea of "intuition" frequently in this book. Intuition is such an essential part of achieving your dreams. And the heart and intuition go hand in hand.

RECOGNIZING THE BEAUTIFUL IN THE IMPERFECT

In your heart of hearts, you know who you are. Deep inside your heart, you also know that you are good enough – even with all your faults and failings.

Our society is largely built up around the supposition that everything has to be perfect. Our lives have to be perfect, our children have to be perfect and have to behave perfectly. Many people wear themselves out, laboring through a hectic workday, only to follow it up by dragging themselves off to some sport or fitness center in order to achieve the perfect body and perfect state of health. Our friendships must be perfect, and so, too, must our marriages. Everything in life, in fact, has to be perfect as far as possible. I believe that we are simply chasing an illusion, and no matter how fast we run after it or try to achieve it, it will never come true.

I don't know about you but I am, without any doubt whatsoever, my own worst critic in just about any area you can name. To name just one, for instance, I am 100% aware of which parts of my body are somewhat less than perfect. In the past, I used up significant amounts of energy allowing myself to be irritated by my imperfect body. But did it help? Not a bit.

The body is one thing, but attitudes and a whole lifestyle is something else entirely. Over a billion people use Facebook every day. Naturally I am one of them, even though I often ask myself why. When you get right down to it, it is nothing more than a platform for showcasing one's perfect life. The perfect children, perfect spouse, the perfect marriage, the perfect life.

The problem is that we do it without giving it any thought. It simply never crosses our minds that we are striving to create the perfect life but are, in fact, harming both ourselves and those around us. Our norms and cultural guidelines dictate a certain type of behavior which makes us act in ways which we are not even fully aware of every day. This applies both to how we we act towards ourselves and others. And these ways in which we act, are all designed to prop up the illusion of our perfect lives.

I had a conversation with a woman on this very topic during a mentoring session.

All her life she had tried to live up to this "perfect" standard. Speak perfectly, look perfect, be perfect at school, have the perfect career, have the perfect husband, and the perfect family life.

I asked her whether she felt that she did, indeed, have the perfect life and whether she felt that it was the right one for her? She fell silent.

Tears trickled down her cheeks. "No," she answered. The tears flowed more freely as she suddenly realized that everything she was brought up to do and be, which she hated, were the same as what she expected of her son and daughter. She had raised them to strive for and live up to the same level of perfection that she demanded from herself. She had imposed upon them the very same limitations that she had endured, causing terrible damage to not only both of her children, but to all of them in the process.

Throughout her 15-year marriage she had accepted her husband´s need for her to appear perfect in every way, not only in relation to him, but perfect in relation to everyone else around them.

Her perfect appearance, successful career, and attempts to be the perfect mother to their two children were all expressions of what she was expected to live up to, she felt. She had to cook delicious food every day, help with their homework, and, of course, whip up homemade baked treats for the children to take to school when required. All characterized by the same need to strive for and achieve perfection.

The only problem was that it had nothing to do with what was really important to her. It was not something that made her happy, and didn´t contribute to any feelings of happiness in any way. The day I held that session, she decided to change her life. From that moment onwards, she would stop striving to attain something she could never achieve. She had never felt so free before, and so whole.

Through my mentoring sessions, one-on-one, I have, of course, met a great many people who do not feel that they are leading perfect lives, but are nevertheless striving to achieve them. I always ask them why.

It may sound simple, but the perfect life comes through accepting who you are. Not what you are, or what you would like to be, but basically just accepting and loving who you are. You are the greatest gift you will ever receive in your life. You are beautiful as you are with all your shortcomings and imperfections.

I will never win the "Father of the Year" award that´s for sure, because I work all over the world and try to make a difference to as many people as possible. This is my mission. It is an enormous privilege for me to be able to do this, but it also means that I lose out in other ways, as I am not at home as much as I would like to be. But that loss is something I have to live with. For my mission is what makes me a whole person. My mission is one of the things in life that gives me the greatest pleasure, and makes me happy.

 If this makes sense to you, and you are now sitting there wondering what you can do about it – then remember that the only thing standing between today and a whole new day tomorrow, is the decision to change what needs to be changed.

CHAPTER 10

IT IS TIME TO RECAP – HAVE YOU ALREADY BECOME A LITTLE MORE CONSCIOUS?

"Be thankful for what you have.
You will end up having more.
If you concentrate on what
you don´t have, you will never,
ever have enough."

Oprah Winfrey

YOU ARE NOW HALFWAY TOWARDS REACHING YOUR "LIFE BRIDGE" GOAL.
YOUR DREAMS ARE CLOSER THAN EVER BEFORE.

As I mentioned at the beginning of this book, my aim is to help you understand the principles and magic behind "The Life Bridge". To help you understand the mechanisms and principles involved in attracting the things you desire.

Now that we are about halfway through the book, I hope you can say that you have reached the point where you feel that you have become a little more conscious about how you look at things. That you know what I mean when I say that insight provides a perspective on things? I hope so, for I can promise you that wondrous things and bigger dreams are waiting for you at the other end. Just waiting for you to catch up.

In this chapter I would like to recap on a few things. Rewind to a few chapters earlier and remind you of a few essentials. So I can tell that we have reached this point on the journey together?

Let me emphasize something once again. It is SO important that you dare to ask yourself a number of leading questions during your journey. That you dare to reflect on your life along the way.

Who do you spend time with? What direction are you heading in – or would like to? What do you like about what you are doing? And most important of all: why do you choose to spend your time the way you do?

We sometimes feel as though we humans run our lives on autopilot, and just let whatever happens steer our course.

Are you conscious of why you chose the path you took? Did you take it to follow your passion/dream, or to do something you believed you´d enjoy doing? Or did you buckle under to external pressure which delegated you a certain role?

And bearing that in mind – how satisfied are you with your workplace? Your family life? Your romantic relationship? It is important to reflect on these things, on a regular basis, in order to be able to determine what is best for you. What you can contribute most to your own, and to other´s, quality of life. Some people think that because they have to pay the bills, they have to put up with a job they don´t like much. That that´s "just the way things are". Obviously, you have to pay the bills, but don´t let yourself become a slave to it. That is what is important.

DO YOU PRACTICE BEING GRATEFUL FOR WHAT YOU HAVE?

I can´t repeat this enough. Another important part of the process involved in moving from the unconscious to the conscious is: "not taking things for granted".

Even the most basic things in life shouldn´t be taken for granted. Once you begin thinking about the many privileges we are surrounded by, your awareness of this will begin to expand. This means that you will begin to see things from more than one perspective. Every element of your life is precious and should be appreciated. No matter what you feel grateful for in your life, you ought to be sending it positive energy and love. Whether it is planet Earth, your family, the forest, your house, your garden or the deli around the corner. Not taking things for granted means that we can give back more to those around us, and develop empathy for those who are struggling simply to attain the things we are fortunate enough to enjoy and appreciate every day.

That is why it is important not to take things for granted.

In our daily lives, we tend to take for granted that certain persons or services are or will always be there.

We mustn't forget to forget to be grateful for them. For the little things and big things alike that make our days run smoothly. These actions, these people that help keep things running on a day-to-day basis, must not become things or people we just expect to be there, doing what they do – presuming they will always be there.

The main thing to remember here is that positive thinking will, very probably, lead to a more positive mindset, and will influence your actions. Face-to-face contact is another aspect of not taking things for granted that is worth mentioning. If you try and rid yourself of the assumption that everyone understands your style of communicating and your point of view, then it is more likely that you will find yourself able to get your viewpoints across in a way that includes everyone. This benefits everyone involved in the discussion in a positive way.

So far, so good. Live in the present (and be grateful) was one of the important axes, one of the essential elements in the "The Life Bridge" model. Can you remember the other element? Yes, precisely. Your dreams. The core and essence of your dreams. And – as mentioned previously – inner self awareness – knowing what you really want – is absolutely essential if you want to be able to feel what your wishes and dreams are. So I would like to share my thoughts with you on being your authentic self. Being true to yourself. Listening to your authentic self is where being true to yourself begins.

CHAPTER 11

THE AUTHENTIC SELF

THE CLOSER YOU GET TO YOUR AUTHENTIC SELF – THE CLOSER YOU ARE TO REALIZING YOUR DREAM

You deserve EVERYTHING you wish for. And probably, your authentic self will burn even more brightly than you imagine once you begin to listen to your dreams and wishes.

Personally, I can recognize only too well that sense of wanting something so badly I can almost taste it, only to have that feeling disappear again. I am also familiar with the well-meaning advice that is dished out on how to achieve success. BUT I also know why those strategies don´t always work.

Following good advice is seldom the route to success when pursuing your dream. Genuine success that you have earned, comes from following what your authentic self tells you to do, not by listening to other people´s way of doing things. Listen to your own voice, first and foremost. What do YOU feel you should do?

Outside influences don´t always work on inner conflicts!

The right path for YOU – the one that will lead you in the right direction and get you moving – is the one that lets you listen to your inner voice. All you have to do is to turn your gaze inwards and find the answer within yourself: What is YOUR authentic self telling you? What would make YOU happy?

It sounds almost unbelievable, but it is absolutely true.

The moment you start to synchronize your inner voice with your actions – then quite magical things begin to happen, and you will start to live the life you can only dream of right now. And do you know what?

The day this dawns on you, is the day you will begin to really relish this journey of growth that you have started out on. That much I promise you.

And I also promise you that you will experience life more intensely, more genuinely, and more colorfully, free of filters or numbing mechanisms.

Try taking a break from your thoughts. Try and switch off for a moment. Do some meditation – perhaps a heart meditation – and notice how you escape from your thoughts. Instead, it is your body, your intuition, your inner voice that you are practicing listening to. This takes practice – that´s for sure! But practice makes perfect, and it is yet another step on the path to fulfilling your dreams.

Listen to, and feel, what is inside, for that is where the answer lies. What makes you happy? And how can you reach that point? You heart, your authentic self, holds the answer.

ARE YOU TRUE TO YOUR OWN CORE VALUES? ARE YOU THE PERSON YOU WANT TO BE?

We all have a set of core values that, deep down inside, we yearn to follow. A yearning we strive to satisfy. Our set of values is based on who we really are – in behind the façade, the rules, the habits, and the noise that surrounds us. So when we begin to compromise on our set of values, then we also settle for something less than our authentic self. And when we do this, we begin to experience an inner turmoil. A warning light tells us that we are not living up to who we really are, and to what we really want for ourselves. The values and our authentic self are linked to each other, you see. Therefore, it is also clear that you need to ask yourself deep down inside: "What are my core values? Am I living up to them? Do I feel that I am following those values – my authentic self?"

To do this, you must look at the choices you have made in life, and those you haven´t, one more time. You must examine all areas of your life honestly, look yourself in the eye in the mirror and ask: "Do I choose according to my own core values?"

It takes courage and hard work to examine these things. But it is necessary if you want to move forward. If you want to discover what you truly dream of, if you really want to identify the kind of life you want to live. And, actually, as luck would have it, your authentic self can help you out here. For your authentic self is itself your *blueprint*. It is who you really are inside. What you were born as. And it is here, that your potential lies.

CHAPTER 12

USE YOUR INTUITION

"You can ask the universe for all the signs you want. But ultimately, we see what we want to see when we´re ready to see it."

MAKE FRIENDS WITH YOUR INTUITION – YOU ARE GOING TO NEED IT

We humans are equipped with one of the most advanced and amazing tools, one that has developed further with each life that is lived.

This tool is our intuition. The ability to be able to know instinctively what feels right, and what feels wrong.

Intuition is also what most of us call "gut feeling". This gut feeling or intuition is one of the most advanced tools we humans possess. Yet at the same time, it is also one of the purest and most primitive.

My assertion is that when we look around us and see what a complex world we live in today – in our personal lives as well as our working lives – then you can usually trace back to the root of it. But why did things become so complicated? Was it the moment we, as humans, stopped believing in ourselves, and trusting and following our intuition?

To be able to use that intuition, you also need to be able to connect to your true self, and what you feel. For if you cannot feel anything, then how can you listen to your intuition?

The intuitive person is also the strongest person, for the intuitive person is able to navigate their way through an ever-changing world, and will also be able to do so in the future. To be able to believe in, count on and work with this does, however, require that we stop and take some time-out.

Why do so many people practice extreme sports? Ironman, 10 marathons a year, off-piste skiing, and so on?

My theory is that most of these people do it because it is the only time they where they could really feel anything.

When the adrenaline is pumping so hard that the body is protesting in pain, that's when they feel like their true selves and most alive.

During my mentoring sessions with people who practice extreme sports, they have confirmed that once they realized this, through having gained a deeper understanding of themselves, they were then able to relax on a couch or in the sauna. Calmly – without fidgeting about. And were able to connect with their feelings. Before they practically had to bike vertically up a mountainside in order to feel anything at all.

The crucial point here is to find a method that lets you get in touch with your intuition, whatever that may be. What will it take for you to hear it? What external noise do you need to get rid of in your life before you can hear it? We discussed this briefly earlier on. People numb their lives with things like working too hard, alcohol, dysfunctional relationships, chasing after material goods, and so on. Slapping on a plaster makes it difficult for your intuition to get a word in. It is quite simply drowned out. Therefore, you must be prepared to remove the noise, rip off the plaster. Your intuition wants the very best for you. It is your voice, your soul that is calling.

USE YOUR INTUITION IN YOUR DAILY LIFE

Think of your intuition as a valued counselor who has your best interests at heart. In all aspects of your life and daily existence. Both in your personal life as well as your working life. We don't do ourselves any favors by ignoring our own signals and personal boundaries in our daily lives, but this is where our intuition comes to our rescue. This might be, for example, when something is telling you to follow a certain course concerning a client, a job you have to do, or something similar – so why not listen to that feeling? Maybe the figures and statistics indicate something else, but what would happen if you followed your intuition instead? You would probably find that other people would be able to understand your way of thinking, your analysis of the situation – because here's the interesting thing about intuition: very often, we all have the same feeling that we can't explain. Likewise this could apply to things like romantic relationships, friendships and family relationships. Intuition is incredibly good at guiding us through the relationships we are involved in. How we perceive each other. How we talk to each other. And not least of all: in those face-to-face conversations when we know, because our intuition is telling us, that the person might be telling us one thing, but really means something else.

YOUR INTUITION ALWAYS TELLS THE TRUTH – BUT YOUR THOUGHTS DO NOT

Sometimes our thoughts play games with us. For example, we may be afraid in certain situations; afraid that we won't succeed at a particular task, afraid that we might be rejected by our partner. That fear – those thoughts – go round and around in our head. This is the ego talking. When the ego overrules our intuition, we sometimes make the wrong decisions. We are afraid, for example, in situations where we don't need to be afraid. That's why it is often much better to listen to your intuition instead of your thoughts (the ego). Because intuition doesn't lead us astray. Our thoughts, however, do every once in awhile.

For me, intuition is enormously important when we talk about dreams and goals in life. For intuition is a tool that can be of tremendous assistance in our lives. It is the thread that links the elements of our life's journey – our life game plan – if you wish to live a meaningful life in harmony with your authentic self, your energy and your whole being.

CHAPTER 13

WHAT IS ENERGY?

"Positive energy
can heal the universe."

UNDERSTANDING ENERGY

I have mentioned energy several times in the course of this book. Now it´s time to take a closer look at it. The unbelievable force that cannot be seen, but can be felt and sensed. The incredible and uplifting energy that can help you on your way. The force of energy that flows throughout our lives.

The word energy is used in a number of different contexts. For some, it means electricity and the natural resources that create energy such as thunder and lightning.

For others, it represents enthusiasm and the will to succeed at something. When you feel energetic, you feel like doing something creative or playing a sport. Here, the word energy represents something rather more abstract. It is a quality that exists in different things: places, situations, people, thoughts, ideas, actions, words, etc. Energy is something everyone can feel, when we are in a state of balance. Energy can be felt as a physical sensation in the body. Depending on the situation, it will manifest itself in different places. Negative energy can often be felt as an aching in the chest, or tightness in the neck or you may notice that you feel cold.

Strong, positive energy, on the other hand, can be felt as lightness in the body and a feeling of inner warmth. The feelings are not 100 % the same for everyone. Nevertheless, we should be able to feel the energy and work with it, if we are observant and notice how we and others around us are feeling.

When I try to describe it, it may sound a little abstract, but I am quite sure that you have experienced these feelings yourself plenty of times. Energy, both our own energy, and that of others, affects us all.

Haven´t you ever noticed that some people you spend time with always seem to lift your spirits and make you happy? Or the opposite – that some people drag you down? It could be a work colleague, a friend, or a member of the family. Or maybe you've also felt completely drained after a hard day's work, until you get together with a friend who always lightens your mood? This is human energy at work, influencing your feelings. We are constantly under the influence and affected by the energies around us, and the connections we form.

Relationships between people are what make the world go round. When we spend time with people who share the same kind of energy that we have, we connect in a unique way. We create a synergy between us which enables each individual involved to feel how the other people are feeling. This means that unique groups can be formed in which we can share and create special situations, dreams and fantastic results. The interesting thing about energy is that is the purest connection between two people. Your energy can connect to someone you appear to have almost nothing in common with, or with someone from a completely different generation. But if you are on the same wavelength energy-wise, a connection at some basic human level, will allow you to share joys and sorrow, and gain a deep understanding of each other.

YOUR INTUITION IS LINKED TO ENERGY

When you use your intuition, you will feel energized. When you use your intuition to make a decision, or you react or say something in a particular way, you are sensing the possible outcomes in the energy, and have chosen the one which contained the strongest energy. You feel it and communicate this to the outside world. Have you never listened to someone talking who seems to be saying all the right things? Their body language backs up what they are saying, but somehow you get the feeling, in some way or another, that something is not quite right. This is because you can sense the energy, and feel that something isn't quite as it should be.

In other words, energy is everything.

It is all around us, in what we see/feel, we share it with other people, and it is what we are made of. That is why our feelings have a direct impact on our energy and vice versa. If we have a positive attitude and, therefore, positive feelings and thoughts, then our energy levels will be high. This will translate into positive actions and intentions. In addition, the energy in our surroundings: our environment, the people, the places, etc. will also have an impact on our feelings. If we often find ourselves surrounded by low energy, then we will be dragged down, too, and have fewer positive feelings.

As mentioned before, places also possess different energies which come from the people who have passed through them, and the things that have happened there through the ages. If we visit a site where joyful historic events have been celebrated, then we will most likely experience positive and dynamic energy. We will feel the positive energy that was present at that time. Similarly, the energy in places where something unpleasant has happened will feel clingy and uncomfortable. These two examples may make it easier for us to relate to how situations, people, thoughts, actions, etc. possess energy.

It is important to be aware of your own energy. What kind do you emit? Similarly, it is just as important to learn how to sense where the right kind of energy is. The energy that matches your dreams. When you find yourself in a situation in which you need to make a decision, you need to be able to feel whether what you decide matches the energy of your dreams, or not.

WHY IS ENERGY IMPORTANT?

Why is it so important to be able to feel the energy? The answer is: Trust and respect.

In the course of pursuing our dreams, we are often confronted with a great deal of uncertainty. We can't always be sure just what the right decision is. But by noticing the type of energy that is present – and the types of feelings the dream arouses in us, we will be better informed when the time comes to make that decision.

FEEL OTHER PEOPLE´S ENERGY

If we surround ourselves with people who have the same type of energy as us, the synergy will become much stronger. It will enable us to work more closely together and reach a common understanding as a group, a couple, etc. This happens because we share the same energy field. Our minds and souls are linked together.

Energy is present in everything and everyone. Before you can feel it and work with it, however, you need to remove some rather complex layers. By drawing on your own feelings and energy, you will be able to see through these complex layers and outside influences, and feel whether the energy is good or bad.

This does not imply that you should disregard all other grounds upon which a decision could be based, but when you are unsure which way to go, being able to sense the energy is a fantastic tool to have. It then becomes a question of whether that decision feels right or not.

Similarly, when we enter an energy field from the outside, we get a certain feeling. For example, take the case of a group of people who have been together for a long time. Here, we will be able to feel the group´s energy. If the energy is negative, we will feel drained. Perhaps we will begin to have negative thoughts, something which we didn´t have before we joined the group. If you are not aware of what is causing these negative influences, in all probability, your subconscious will pick up on it and, later on, it will surface in your conscious thoughts.

The opposite can also happen, where you meet a lively group who raise your energy levels so you feel more inspired and more positive. When that happens, you are connecting so you the same feelings. You will also be more inclined to develop more positive energy. You will get new ideas, create more synergy, and be more inspired.

And then there is neutral energy. When you run into neutral energy, it will have no effect on you. In this state, the energy that surrounds you is neither good nor bad. And you will not actually be aware of when this occurs. Neutral energy means that you are not consciously able to feel or attract the things you would like. You will be more influenced by those around you, who don't really care one way or the other about what you want. This is not necessarily because they wish you any harm, but they won't help you either. Nothing will happen. You'll find yourself running on the spot. Many people possess this kind of energy, which is interesting if you look at the potential that would be realized if only these people expanded their awareness of their own energy and began to attract their dreams.

What about you? Are you aware of the various types of energy you come into contact with? And the type of energy you emit yourself?

RAISE YOUR ENERGY LEVELS

One thing that gives people positive energy is having something that gives some meaning to their lives. Finding a purpose in what they do – whether it adds meaning to their own lives, or the lives of others. Whatever it is, it must mean something to you personally. It could simply be feeling good about the task you are doing, or the feeling of well-being you get from helping a member of the family. Finding a purpose in the things you do will get you far, as it is one of the most satisfying things in life. So find out what will give meaning to your life – and do it!

Another way of raising your energy levels and motivation in life is to set specific goals.

These do not have to be work-related. Making a list of specific things you want to achieve can help you focus your energy on a few, selected activities. This will help you get better results because there is more focus on the energy. Have a brainstorming session on all the things/experiences/activities you would like to improve on, or have in your life. Pick five from the list and focus on them until you achieve them. These successes – small as well as large – can have a great impact on raising energy levels. I am sure that almost everyone, at some time in their life, has experienced a boost in their energy levels when they achieve something that matters to them. But it is important to remember that a true increase in your energy level only happens when you succeed at something that is important to *you* – not to those around you.

IS THERE ENERGY IN MONEY?

Some people get an enormous amount of energy from making money and having plenty of it.

Money is not everything, but it is very nice to have. Money equals freedom.

For me, money is a tool. A tool, a means to an end that I use to live out some of my dreams. Those dreams, that is, in which money is one of the pieces of the overall jigsaw puzzle.

During my own personal journey, and during many of the conversations I have had with other people, I have noticed a big difference between the people who make their dreams come true – and those who don´t. Their attitude towards money, and the way they relate to it, is a crucial factor in their ability to attract money.

So what exactly do I mean by money being just a tool? I mean that if you put the act of making money before the desire to achieve your dream, then you will limit your ability to attract that dream, because there is NO energy in money itself.

If you want to attract your dreams, you need energy. The more you work on improving the quality of your dreams, the more energy you will put into them. This is the reinforcing element that will send a clear signal to the universe which will, in turn, give back by providing the supportive energy you need. These combined energies will make the distance between your starting point and your future destination (your dream) shorter and shorter.

On one condition – and that is that you must remember that you cannot control time – and that having doubts will block your energy to just as great an extent. The same thing applies if you start focusing on why you are not making money during the process of attracting your dream.

Money is only a tool, and it will come to you if you just remember to ask the universe to help you live out your dreams.

CHAPTER 14
THE LIFE BRIDGE MODEL

"The best way to predict your future is to create it."

Abraham Lincoln

YOUR DREAMS ARE ABOUT TO COME TRUE. ARE YOU READY?

It´s no coincidence that I have waited until now to delve deeper into "The Life Bridge Model".

Well, actually, this whole book is about the model. About understanding how it can help you to achieve the life you dream of. But I don´t think you were ready to understand the reasoning behind it before now – am I right? Now you are ready. Readier than ever, I sense.

I have mentioned this previously in the book. We all have dreams, goals and wishes for our future. Things we would like to achieve, things we would like to have. Perhaps you dream of getting a new job, of moving house, of having a boyfriend or girlfriend, of traveling more – or of simply being happy and contented when you wake up every morning.

It is only natural and part of being human to want more. To have ambition, to expect to have more or be more than what we have or are now.

Many of us also walk around longing for something inside. A longing we can´t really define, but which we believe will somehow be fulfilled if only we get those things we dream about. If we just reach our goal.

Perhaps this longing is a question of wanting to return to what you once were – when you were born. Perhaps you can recall a time when life was great, carefree and the world lay at your feet? Just what was it that made you feel that way? Some people might answer:

"I had just fallen in love, I had a good job, lived in a great place, had loads of friends, was young, was making a lot of money", and so forth.

But that is one of the traps the mind lays for us. Because there is nothing out there in the future that can make you happier or more successful –

UNLESS YOU ARE GRATEFUL AND APPRECIATE THE LIFE YOU HAVE, HERE AND NOW.

If you take responsibility for the life you have today – and understand that the path to happiness, the dream or success that you desire is a process, that starts when you accept and live the life you are living today. Then and only then, will you understand the balance, the entire concept behind "The Life Bridge".

In my experience, as long as we ONLY continue to search for something outside ourselves, detached from ourselves and completely different from the life we are living today – then that sense of longing will never disappear. And it is that sense of longing that tilts our life out of balance and makes us unhappy.

And, even more importantly, as I as I previously stated: In order to have your dreams fulfilled, you must first of all learn to love, honor and be grateful for all the good things you already have in your life. For if you focus exclusively on the things you would like to have – but don´t have yet – then you will end up dissatisfied, and in a state of imbalance in the here and now. And this state will certainly not attract all the good things you wish for in your life. In other words, your energy will be out of kilter. There will be precious little energy left for the good things, the new things.

My view is that if you focus on all the good things in your life, everything that is going well for you here and now – then it will be much easier for you to achieve all the things you dream of.

If you focus on everything you don´t have – you will throw everything off balance.

THE LIFE BRIDGE MODEL

The heart (the here and now) and the cloud (your dreams for the future) must be in balance. A state of equilibrium must exist between your present and your future so that you can navigate and feel who you really are. The life you have here and now should be cherished and taken seriously – EVEN if you desire other, new things in your future life. Of course, you can dream! Dream big and believe it will happen – but don´t dream at the expense of the here and now. The key word here is balance between the two. Yes, that´s right – the heart and the cloud. The heart and the cloud in your "Life Bridge" must be in a state of absolute equilibrium.

Let me elaborate a little on what we mean by "The Life Bridge Model".

At first glance, when you look at the heart and the cloud and the bridge that links them, you are probably wondering what on earth it all means?

The heart represents the level of awareness (consciousness) we have of all the things we should love and be grateful for here in our present lives – here and now. The cloud symbolizes the dream(s) you might like to have, and the bridge is basically just the energy that connects these two elements.

This energy is what I have used subconsciously all my life, and use consciously today, to attract my most of my dreams. Twenty-four hours a day, seven days a week, people, companies, and every element in our lives receive energy. A universal energy that comes from outside ourselves, and this also applies when we dream, because it is the energy that attracts our dreams.

Every day we enter into a type of multi-dimensional "space" filled with energy, where the energy circulates around these two elements – the heart and the dream. This energy is the bridge that connects our present with the future we desire.

Imagine an old-fashioned scale. You need to balance these two elements – the heart on one side and your dreams (symbolized by a cloud) on the other. In my view,
these are the two cornerstones of life. This is the "equation" that creates balance. For this illustrates an awareness that if we focus too much, or not at all, on achieving our dreams, then the feeling of happiness we enjoy in the present will disappear. And conversely, if we only channel our focus and energy into our present, then we will miss out on all the opportunities that are waiting for us in the future.

In my experience, many people get stuck in the past. They are waiting for the future to happen, but forget to live now. As P.J. Parrish says in "The Killing Song":

"If you put one foot in the past, and one foot in the future, the only thing left to do is piss on the present." This is basically what the "Life Bridge" model will help you change. If we get stuck in the past instead of learning from it, then we will never move on; will never reach the future or even the present, for that matter.

We cannot define the route to our goal before we have reached it. And this is where most people, and most companies, go wrong. For when a company works with its strategy, it focuses on the route to that goal. It tries to define the direction in which it must head to reach that goal. And when we do that, in principle, it is the equivalent of removing the bridge (the energy) and replacing it with a tunnel to connect the heart and cloud. Now instead of having a route (bridge) that allows the energy to flow freely and have a positive effect on everything, we end up with a limited form of energy as we are now forcing it through a tunnel that greatly restricts its flow.

If we then begin to introduce milestones as well, this is the equivalent of filling up the tunnel with more material. So we go from having a limitless "room" of high-level energy to an energy that is greatly weakened. The bridge takes longer to cross. This means that the heart (the present) and the cloud (the dream) are pushed farther apart. Thus, the weakened energy reduces your ability to achieve your goals, the ability to attract what you dream of. We need to respect the fact that things take time. In other words: We must let go – stop trying to control things and stop managing this process, and have faith that the energy will find its own way, the right way, in due time.

CHAPTER 15
THE PATH TO VISUALIZATION

"Never give up on a dream
just because of the time
it will take to accomplish it.
The time will pass anyway."

Earl Nightingale

HOW DO WE VISUALIZE OUR DREAMS?

There is no doubt that being able to visualize right down to the smallest detail on your journey, plays a big part in defining and attracting your dreams, and is one of the most essential elements involved in making them come true.

Visualizing things also sharpens our focus. The ability to visualize something in its entirety is something that has helped me greatly, and has helped those I have guided through the same exercise.

Visualization can be used in virtually any situation. You can use it to get a better overview of the tasks you have to do. You can use it when you are going through a challenging time in your life, when you are feeling a little down. It can help you focus on the things that make you happy instead.

A 'Happy board', as I call it, is something that can be really useful here and make a big difference. Filling it with pictures that illustrate all the things that make you happy, will also help you discover and define what exactly what these things are more precisely. It could be your children, your spouse. It could be chocolate, ice cream, or going for a walk or a run. It might be travelling, meditating, or listening to music. It is whatever you feel makes you happy. And the process of finding these pictures is in itself highly stimulating and increases your inner love and happiness.

WHAT HAPPENS WHEN WE VISUALIZE?

Visualization is a method of picturing ourselves in the dream scenario. By this we mean, allowing ourselves to experience the physical emotions that would arise if we found ourselves in the individual situations we have visualized.

Some people relate to "visual" stimuli better than others. If you are one of these people, instead of looking for actual pictures, try writing down your thoughts and describing the pictures you imagine instead of searching for them, if this works better for you. One thing that is important to remember if you choose to "visualize" using words, is to let go and just let the words flow. In other words, don´t expend too much energy on analyzing whether or it is right or wrong or not. Don´t start worrying about whether you should have chosen something else instead, something "better". No, this is an exercise in taking things as they come, and letting your intuition guide you.

BE SPECIFIC WHEN YOU VISUALIZE

When you are just beginning the dream process, that´s when it is the most difficult to get down to details.

For example, it is not enough to say "I´d like to travel". Fair enough, but where do want to go? The world is your oyster when it comes to going off exploring new territory. It is important to define where you want to go, and when. Above all, what is the higher purpose behind your desire to travel?

Explore and define your dream in greater detail and say something like,"I would like to visit Europe".

Great! Which countries in Europe?

"Hadn´t thought about it."

OK, let´s start again.

" I would like to visit Europe."

Why England instead of France?

"I don´t know."

Hmm, not really getting anywhere, are we? Visualization/articulating what we want has to be specific, for example:

"I would like to go to London. I´d like to go in April when they hold the London Marathon which I´ve always dreamed of running in."

Getting right down to the details and being specific about when things should happen, and why – that´s the key. How the dream actually turns out is very important at this stage of the visualization process. For once you get this far, then you will also be able to find the images you need to visualize the dream itself.

CHAPTER 16

THE UNIVERSE IS LISTENING

"Follow your bliss and
the universe will open doors
where there were only walls."

Joseph Campbell

THE UNIVERSE HEARS YOU.
PRACTICE LISTENING TO WHAT IT TELLS YOU.

One of the reasons the universe exists is to accommodate your wishes.

If you believe in and wish for something deep inside, with no trace of doubt or fear, then the universe will work with you on achieving it. This does not mean, however, that you can simply lean back and wait for it to materialize. It means that the universe will point you in the right direction. Towards what you want to achieve. It will help you create energy and interaction in the circumstances you are in which will, in turn, propel you towards where you really want to be.

This makes pretty good sense if you think about it. If you are 100% convinced that you will achieve something, and put in the time and effort that it takes, then you will succeed. Part of that 100% includes taking a bold approach towards your goal. When you set a goal without fear or doubt, you will experience a physical sensation of calm when you think about achieving that goal. Once you reach the point where you are certain that this is the goal for you, then the universe will take note and help you reach it. By this, I mean that opportunities will open up for you; you will meet certain people, find yourself in the right place or situation, and will understand these as pointers of some kind that will help you on your journey towards your goal.

You still have to work hard, but you will feel like you have been "fortunate" with how things have turned out. And that is the reason why we shouldn´t carry the burden of doubt and fear around with us, but should try to remain tranquil and feel secure and confident. Believe that you can achieve what you wish for and dream of. And have FAITH that your dreams will come true when the time is right.

Perhaps the answer to your dreams will arrive in a different guise, in a slightly different way or version than you had imagined. But the opportunity and the answer will arrive. So when you find yourself in a situation in which you have to make an important decision, check whether your emotions could have some part to play in that decision-making process. Does it feel right?

I have learned that the universe's timing is always spot on, and experiences I have had and continue to have in my own life regularly confirm this. But knowing that the timing is perfect is one thing, knowing how to interpret and listen to the messages you receive is quite another.

Sometimes it is hard to know what the right choice is. This is why I can't emphasize enough how important it is to practice getting in touch with your intuition. When something instinctively feels right, you will feel your whole body relax completely. Conversely, you will experience a feeling of restlessness if you act out of sync with your intuition.

For deep, deep down inside, you know the right answer.

CHAPTER 17

WHAT YOU SHOULD KNOW ABOUT TIME

"Time you enjoy wasting,
was not wasted."

John Lennon

YOU CANNOT CONTROL TIME

Time is a strange concept. How you perceive time depends on what you are doing, who you are with, and where you are. We cannot even control the amount of time we will spend here on earth. And we cannot, for instance, control when things will happen.

When we dream and work with our "Life Bridge", it is important to disregard the concept of time because it is virtually impossible to predict when our dreams will come true. Only when one of your dreams has come true, will you be able to pinpoint how long it took, and see how everything related to each other. The point is that you must never give up even if you don´t know when you will succeed. Keep working towards achieving your dream without stressing yourself out by setting a time limit, as this will only create turbulence in your energy in the form of doubt or pressures that may have an impact on the dream.

One of the reasons that the amount of time used to achieve our dreams is an unpredictable factor is that many other factors, apart from your own efforts and input, also play a role in the process. Therefore, the simplest approach to time is simply to acknowledge that you have no control over it. You will have to do your best to attract as much positive energy as possible to yourself and your dreams, and let the universe help you. For if we focus too much on time, then we may lose sight of what is really important in what we are doing, and thus miss out on some opportunities because we have been focusing on the wrong things. By this, I mean that if you only focus on keeping to a schedule, then you won´t see what is happening around you.

If, on the other hand, you let time take care of itself, and focus instead on the elements and purpose of your dream, you´ll realize after awhile that the process will run much more smoothly this way. Learning to stop worrying about time is, therefore, very important.

GIVE YOURSELF TIME TO DREAM

We all lead hectic lives. But if we want to grow, want to work on achieving our dreams, then we need to devote time to them. In between our daily routines and goals, it is important that we take time out to dream. Take a minute to visualize our dreams during our daily commute to and from work, jot them down on a scrap of paper, or put aside a couple of hours a day to work on our dreams. This may vary from person to person. But learning to make good use of the time you have, and being aware of how we use our time, is a "must" in relation to achieving those dreams. Your time is valuable, so it is important to reflect on how you use it, and whether or not you are satisfied with how you use it.

As I have mentioned a couple of time already, balance is the key word in working with your "Life Bridge".

In regards to time, the challenges you face will be no different. As I have said, it is a good idea to be aware of how you use your time, and whether or not you use it in a way that relates to your dream. At the same time, however, it is equally important not to become a slave to planning. If you do, you will lose some of your creative energy because you will be constantly focusing on deadlines, on whether or not you are going to make it in time, with whatever you are doing. You need to introduce an element of calm, to give yourself time to think creative thoughts, and to give your mind and soul the opportunity to reflect on things that have happened. Following a strict schedule only narrows your field of vision and limits your sense of freedom.

It´s a good idea to allow yourself an hour or two every day, or half a day per week or every other week, in which nothing has been scheduled. Then you will be able to use that time on whatever feels right at that moment, but it must be something that allows you to look inwards and reflect on what it is that gives your life meaning.

THE PAST, THE PRESENT AND THE FUTURE

Another important factor is the link between the past, the present, and the future. We must realize that in order to attract the future, we need to live in the present. How we act, how we react, and the things we do now are precisely the things that define our future. Instead of constantly focusing on the distant future, find out what you want in your life, focus on and enjoy the present moment, and work towards the future. The only things that exist are the things that are real here and now – nothing else. The past has come and gone – and we must learn to accept it and let go. As for the future, well, it hasn´t arrived yet, and what defines the future is the present – so make the most of it. As they say, "The present is a gift, so enjoy it!"

We cannot control time, but we can choose how we use it. And we do this by using it on something that adds meaning to our lives.

Many people find it hard to live in the present. Advances in technology and the social media constantly encourage us to record/capture the moment in photos/ and write about the present – instead of actually *living* that moment 100% here and now, while we are in it. In addition, we are constantly bombarded with events and opportunities which tends to make us feel that we mustn´t miss out on anything. We join in relentlessly. No matter what it is, we´ll be there. We work full-time while raising our children, work out, entertain at home, or attend other people´s parties, and on and on. All these things are fun, but we need to learn to accept that we can´t do all of these things all at the same time, and if we do, then we will not really be fully present at half of them. And that creates an imbalance.

HOW WOULD YOU LIKE TO USE YOUR TIME?

According to researchers, we live 25,915 days on average. If we then calculate that we sleep an average of 7.5 hours per night, this means we spend 194,365 hours sleeping.

Therefore, we are awake for approximately 621,960 hours during our lifetimes. (Source: http://bigthink.com/paul-ratner/how-many-days-of-your-life-do-you-have-sex-your-lifetime-by-the-numbers)

Shouldn't we then make sure that we put these hours to very good use? Don't let your present pass you by. The past used up just a fraction of these hours, there is plenty of time left to enjoy the present. Looking at our lives from the viewpoint of time makes us more consciously aware of precisely what we want to invest our time in. A large part of "The Life Bridge" deals with just that – living life wholeheartedly in the present. This is a large part of what balance is all about.

CHAPTER 18

THE POWER IN ASKING FOR HELP

"Prayer is the key of the morning
and the bolt of the evening."

Mahatma Gandhi

ASK THE UNIVERSE FOR HELP

I firmly believe that the universe helps us achieve our goals and wishes. One of the things I think is worth spending time on is asking the universe for help, asking for help from something outside ourselves. For myself personally, this means asking for help, and making contact with something that is greater than myself. Sending my wishes and dreams out to the energies that I believe can help me along the way. Saying what I wish for out loud. Letting the universe hear me.

Asking for help really does work. Asking for help has a powerful effect. You will be surprised to find that when you ask the universe for help – it will answer you. It is as if you set a wheel in motion that puts you on the right track. As if you are suddenly no longer alone with your wishes.

ASKING FOR HELP IS A POWERFUL TOOL

Personally, I have no doubt whatsoever that asking for help works. Can I prove it to you and convince you? *I* probably can´t, but many scientific studies and countless personal anecdotes can illustrate how people have been helped by – and found greater tranquility and purpose - through asking for help, or what some call prayer.

Asking for help also works when you are upset, unhappy, discouraged, worried or struggling with other emotions that are weighing you down. Asking for help may have a comforting, soothing, uplifting effect, or may provide you with a new outlook on the problem. Or it may help you to see what needs to be done before you can take the next step along your journey´s path.

Asking for help let´s you open your heart, shed light on your soul, and see your own worth, beauty and importance.

YOU WILL ALWAYS BE HEARD WHEN YOU ASK FOR HELP.

You must have faith and believe that when you have asked for help, you have been heard. The universe has begun to work on turning those wishes into a reality. Some take longer than others. Something else you must take into consideration is that your wishes must also be what your soul wants, too. I cannot emphasize this enough. As Mark Twain wrote, "You can't pray a lie." If you have asked for an answer to a question, be aware that it may appear in different ways. And remember that your dream may come true in ways in which you might not have imagined.

CHAPTER 19

CONNECTING THE DOTS

"Patience is not the ability to wait – it´s how we behave while we are waiting."

Joyce Meyer

THE METHOD AND PATH CHOSEN ARE OUT OF YOUR HANDS

Let me state this one more time. When you dream of things – set goals and wishes for your life and future – it´s important that you understand that you have no control over how you reach those goals. The way in which those dreams come true cannot be provoked, planned or forced. If you try to do this, you will find to your cost that you will ruin the energy – challenge the universe – and that´s not your job. Your task is to have faith in, and believe in, the universe and the process.

I mentioned previously that Steve Jobs once held a keynote speech at Stanford University, in which he talked about "connecting the dots."

The expression "connecting the dots" was used here to illustrate that when we dream and set goals for ourselves, it is fine to identify the elements we´d like included in those dreams, as long as we understand that we cannot control the path these dreams follow on the way to being realized. We can search for the dream. We can attract it and influence it using our focus and energy. But it is only once we have achieved our dream, that we can look back with hindsight and identify the actual path we took to reach it.

In other words, let go of your desire to be in control.

CONTROL IS BASED ON FEAR

The need to control is a deep-seated force in all of us. In our day-to-day life, control provides the the focus that is needed to build up a career, or see the whole picture – or meet the challenges we face along the way. But control gets in the way when you want to relax, just live your life and enjoy the present. This is because the desire to control things is really rooted in fear, and when you are afraid, it takes over completely. And when this happens, you can no longer enjoy life or live in the present.

I am a big fan of patience. For when you are patient, that's when you let things happen all by themselves. Things take time, as we all know. Change takes time. You are on a journey and your destination – your dreams – don't just appear from one day to the next. They will come true when the time is right. Once you have learned that the route to them is about the balance between the present and the future, among other things.

When it comes right down to it, patience plays a vital role in everything, not least of all in the process of developing yourself. Arm yourself with patience along your route. You are steadily progressing from one point to the next on the way to your destination. But change doesn't happen in a week, or even a month. Sometimes, the small steps must mature, before you can move on. And that is when you must tame your impatient streak.

In my experience, we aren't always even consciously aware that we have almost reached our goal. The closer we get to achieving our dream, the more confusing it can become. We can't even see that we are on the right path. Perhaps we can only see all the obstacles that have stood, or still stand, in our way.

But do not let yourself worry. When you are forced into making changes en route, rest assured that better things are also on their way. And I promise you, you'll experience an energy - a rush like no other- the day you realize that one of your dreams has come true.

CHAPTER 20

EVERYTHING IS CONNECTED

"Look around you.
Appreciate what you have.
Nothing will be the same
in a year."

RELAX! YOU ARE A PART OF SOMETHING MUCH BIGGER

I am convinced that everything in life is related. That what we do - or don´t do – has an impact on something else. This also means, of course, that if we are not really aware of what matters in our lives, then we can´t really tell whether we have neglected something or lost something that might have made a difference to our presnt or our future.

Imagine that your life looks like an ordinary wheel on a bike. A wheel with thin spokes. When things are running smoothly, you have all the spokes you need. All you have to do is steer a steady course, go full speed ahead and, most importantly of all, take the bend without breaking any spokes. If, on the other hand, you don´t really know where you are heading, and have little insight into what your life holds, this is the same thing as mounting your bike, and starting off with wheels that have missing or unevenly spaced spokes. So this means you can´t bike fast, you can´t brake very well, and it´s almost impossible to turn. So you have no control whatsoever.

Most people do not realize what their "bicycle wheel" (life) consists of, and therefore, many people find themselves facing the same challenges over and over again. This might include something like getting involved in a relationship with a partner who is the wrong type for you – and no good for you – over and over. But because you are not aware of the factors involved, you repeat the same selection process and end up hurting once again. Or you choose to stay in a job that isn´t good for you, etc.

If you are reading this and it sounds a lot like you, then you can be pretty sure that you are overlooking some signals or needs. This when you should stop and think of the "bicycle wheel". Which "spokes" am I missing that cause my wheel to buckle every time I try to turn, speed up or brake?

These elements have a tendency to repeat themselves in every facet of your life. For example, if things aren't going well at work, this will probably have a knock-on effect at home, and vice versa. If conditions at home are less than ideal, this will almost certainly, have an impact on your work.

ARE YOU YOUR REAL SELF OR JUST PUTTING ON AN ACT?

I am probably not telling you anything you don't already know here. I often find that most people are fully aware that "I am one person at work, and quite another at home!"

In my view, this presents us with somewhat of a dilemma. More like a big conflict, in fact. Because if everything is inter-connected, then it must be extremely difficult, not to say limiting, for a person to consciously/subconsciously choose to "split" themselves up in this way. After all, we are only one person with one body, one soul and one mind. The resources of energy required to maintain two personalities (private versus professional) are hugely depleting. The facade we assume only adds unnecessary complications. Ultimately, you end up distanced from who you really are, and thus limit your own ability to live the life you really want. Your wheel can simply no longer turn around – and you can no longer steer.

You are probably already familiar with this everyday expression. "Accidents rarely happen alone", or we say, or "success attracts success". Good idioms that basically explain the extent to which all things are connected.

WE ARE ALL LINKED TO EACH OTHER

Research has documented that everyone in the whole world is only 6 steps or fewer away from each other!

This means that, as people, we are all linked to each other. It´s a nice thought, but unfortunately, the differences in our behavioral patterns quickly turn the beauty of it into something more complex and obscure, something which is very definitely not attractive at all. The interesting thing is though, that once people begin to appreciate the beauty that lies in being themselves, this is when they will begin to experience how beautiful and meaningful life can be. This comes from having a better understanding of their authentic self. When people connect with other people, in any aspect of life, that´s what strengthens and increases the number of relationships you have. Adds more "spokes to your wheel", if you like. It also means that the strength you gain from being your authentic self, will enable you to tackle greater challenges than you could before. You can say the things you only dared to think and not say before. But wanted to say. And ultimately, you will create and live the life you wished for deep down, either consciously or subconsciously.

CHAPTER 21

YOU CAN MOVE THE PROCESS ALONG

"Accept what is,
let go of what was and
have faith in what will be."

Sonia Ricotti

YOUR JOB IS TO CREATE FLOW

I know that I have said this several times – that you cannot, and should not try, to control the path you take to the dreams you desire. In other words, you must relinquish control, surrender your need to be in charge, and your desire to know everything. BUT, there are several techniques you can use to help you practice this. Techniques that will help you feel the flow, notice the direction, and feel what your heart and intuition are telling you. And you know what? The wonderful thing about it is that the universe will sense your good, positive flow. The universe will be able to feel the field you now move around in – unhindered – which will make it much easier for the universe to fulfill your dreams – faster. More easily and in a purer form.

I have previously touched on meditation as being a fantastic tool for creating inner peace and a state of "thoughtless awareness" in the mind, body and soul. Meditation helps you to feel your inner self – and hear the universe speak. Meditation simply removes all the unnecessary external noise that surrounds you. Positive thinking is another tool that you can actively employ. Do you remember the two important concepts? TIME and PATIENCE? If you practice believing in the process and being patient, then you will be smoothing the path of the flow, both within yourself and around you. In this respect, having faith or believing is the same thing as positive thinking: BELIEVE that things are happening. BELIEVE that you will achieve what you desire. Be positive about your journey, your process.

LET GO – AND YOU WILL RECEIVE

There is another aspect of helping the process along that I would like you to consider:

What is stopping you from creating the life you would like to live right now?

Who or what is stopping you from surrendering yourself to the process?

Yourself?

Your financial situation?

Poor communication between you and your partner?

Your own thoughts, feelings, actions, or experiences from your past life?

Or perhaps you believe that you do not deserve to receive help?

I am willing to bet that the only thing holding you back is yourself. NOW the time has come to let go. NOW is when you should surrender to the process and have faith that everything is under control. There is a plan. You are already well on your way. You have signaled your wishes and dreams. The universe has heard you. Trust in the universe – and the energies – they will do the rest.

CHAPTER 22

LET´S CALL IT THE "PRINCIPLE" OF ATTRACTION

"Create the highest, grandest vision possible for your life, because you become what you believe."

Oprah Winfrey

WHAT YOU THINK, IS WHAT YOU ATTRACT

Now we have reached the last but one chapter of this book. And probably the most important – or one of the most important – if you ask me. The chapter on attraction. How do you attract your dreams? How do you turn all your wishes, goals and dream scenarios into reality? How do you change your life? Let us take a closer look at the concept sometimes referred to as the LAW OF ATTRACTION. A concept I live and breathe for. I can´t wait to share it with you. Are you ready?

Several times I have mentioned that "what you think is what you attract". I have also written about dreams and the fact that you are the only one who sets the limit when it comes to how big you want to dream. But perhaps you have been thinking, "Yes, sounds great! Count me in ! I´d like to dream. I´d like to change my job, find the love of my life, raise adorable children, be financially independent" or whatever it is that you dream of.

As you are already familiar with, your "Life Bridge" consists of two elements: Cherishing the present and embracing your dreams. Fulfilling your dreams isn´t just something that happens overnight, not something you can just snap your fingers and do. So once you have discovered what you truly dream of, how do you go about attracting what you want? How do you get across your "Life Bridge"?

There is an actual defined universal process behind being able to attract dreams. A process I have practiced all my life, yet only became consciously aware of a few years ago. Since then, my dreams have become even more ambitious – and they continue to be fulfilled.

THE THREE UNIVERSAL PRINCIPLES

The tool you will learn about here is based on three universal principles which together make it possible for your dreams to be fulfilled. These three principles are three energy-acceleration points, which must be activated in order to attract whatever you wish for (whether it be big or small). These three principles are:

- *The Principle of Quality*
- *The Principle of Intensity*
- *The Principle of Attraction*

Perhaps you have heard of the book and the movie "Laws of Attraction"? Put simply, it describes how what you think is what you attract. And if you do this, it will happen!

In my view, the problem with this philosophy is that something is missing here. Firstly, it's quite obvious that it doesn't always work, even if you do try to live your life based on these "laws". If it was a true law, then it would work, not just once in awhile, but every single time.

If you introduce any doubt whatsoever into the equation, or neglect to pay time the respect it is due, then the consequences of this are huge: you lose the ability to attract your dreams. This is why I have chosen to describe it as a "principle" rather than a "law".

As demonstrated, there are three steps involved in the process of creating attraction using universal energies. The first point is (1) The Principle of Quality. The next, point (2) is The Principle of Intensity, and the last is the sum of the other two combined, namely point (3) The Principle of Attraction.

When these three principles are set in motion – when synergy is created between their energies – this is when we can succeed in attracting our dreams. It is only yourself, your thoughts, and your beliefs that set the limit.

Your dreams form the point at which balance is achieved on your "Life Bridge". This is the point you need to reach in order to achieve full awareness of what you want to accomplish or have in your life. A conscious awareness of how you will shape your future – rather than just allowing things to happen by chance. Everything happens for a reason, so I don´t believe in coincidences. This also means that if you do not become consciously aware of your two "Life Bridge" elements (LOVE the present, and LOVE your dreams), then you risk becoming "a slave" to your daily grind, your thoughts and behavioral patterns – and basically the life you yourself have created.

In olden days, it was known as slavery. Today we simply call it a state of unconsciousness, to express it in a very simplified way. I believe that far too many people realize too late that they are living a life far removed from the life they dreamed of. A life shaped by the expectations of those around them. This is not the life you deserve, so stop and reflect on what kind of life you would really like – and start building the foundations for it tomorrow. The only thing standing between today and a better day tomorrow, is YOUR decision. You are the most important person in YOUR life.

Let us examine the three principles more closely:

(1) The Principle of Quality

The Principle of Quality deals with being VERY specific about what you want your dream to contain. You need to go into great detail and provide a good explanation as to why you choose some things and reject others.

Dive deeply into your dream – into every detail. The more specific you are, the better it will be.

Let us take the example of your dream job, for instance. A job which you may think, at first glance, is completely out of your reach. Start the dream and visualization process in which you picture yourself in this role. Pay attention to the signals every cell in your body is transmitting – how does it feel? Feel the joy and the pain that goes with being in that job. Let a movie of it run in your imagination, in your mind and soul, where you get a bird´s eye view of yourself. Watch yourself at your desk, writing that job application. Visualize the moment when you press the key and send that e-mail application, or perhaps you´ll decide to deliver your application in person, and have an initial, informal interview. Notice how you feel inside when you visualize these situations in which you specify right down to the smallest detail, how YOU would like things to fit together. Only once you feel that you have gone through every little detail that is significant for you, will you be ready to move on to the next step, The Principle of Intensity.

(2) The Principle of Intensity

Never underestimate how long the process of creating quality and precision in a dream can take. But that is what it takes before you can move on to The Principle of Intensity. This is where the attraction process takes place. Performing the visualization step of the process is always a rewarding task, as this is where you can really get down to defining just precisely what your dreams are.

Working with these types of visualization processes has given me a great deal of pleasure during the last few years, as it enables people to choose the pictures and videos that illustrate the future they desire.

Earlier on in the book, I mentioned this visualization process – the journey of visualization. Personally, I enjoy collecting pictures in a special folder on my cell phone, iPad, computer, etc. I am an avid user of YouTube and follow the things that reinforce my own dreams. Many people might prefer to use a traditional "poster" – a large sheet of paper onto which you can attach actual photos. Every time you get a new dream, add a picture to your visualization process, so that is constantly evolving.

The process involved in The Principle of Intensity is actually where the act of attraction takes place. This is where you can help the energy on your "Life Bridge" to either flow quickly or not as quickly. This is where you can ask for help from the universal energy and *attract* your dreams – rather than chasing *after* them every day.

The Principle of Intensity deals with creating intensity around your dreams. This is where you work on building up energy in your dreams.

If, for example, you have found the house of your dreams, then take a walk around that neighborhood – often. Meet the neighbors, feel the energy in the area. If the house is for sale, read the sales material at the realtor. If they are holding an open house – go along and see what the inside is like, so you can confirm that it really is the perfect house for you. Take a few photos of the house and the neighborhood and look at them, imagine yourself living there. Imagine how you will furnish the house right down to the smallest detail. But remember that even if you work intensively on your dream, there is still one factor you cannot influence.

Be patient – the more you work with the dream, the more intensely the energy will flow to you – and the more powerful the force of attraction will be.

(3) The Principle of Attraction

The Principle of Attraction is actually 1+2 = 3.

This means that provided that you work on following the first two principles, then The Principle of Attraction will take care of itself. For once you have done the work that is needed, the energy will take you the rest of the way.

What I think is most interesting about my own dreams, is that in 98% of them, I am not aware of the fact that my dream is about to come true. Only once I am living it out, do I realize that fact. What´s more, I have also realized that the dream that has now come true is often not the next one on my list, but another somewhere else on that list.

So what is my point? My point is once again that you cannot control time, and you cannot control which dream will come true, or when. But you can have a direct influence on what you want to fill your life with today, and in the future. And this is thanks to your "Life Bridge".

MY OWN DREAMS

Most of my dreams have come true – when the time has been right.

I should also add that when it comes to my own dreams, the list is so long that I have had to shorten it a little and drop a few of those dreams. Does that mean that by the time I die, I reckon all of my dreams will have come true? No, at least I certainly hope not. Dreaming and working on making those dreams come true is a lifelong project – one on which I intend to keep working on for the rest of my life. I find it so meaningful and energizing – working on my dreams, developing them and seeing them turn into reality.

CHAPTER 23

TO CONCLUDE

"Three things you cannot recover in life: the word after it´s said. The moment after it's missed and the time after it´s gone."

Ziad K. Abdelnour

REACHING THE END

We have reached the end of our journey together.

The end of the book, but the beginning of your new life. Full of dreams that will unfold, and doors that will open for you. There is light at the end of the tunnel. Plenty of light. I hope that the journey so far has benefitted you. That you have learned something, become a little braver, and can see the way ahead more clearly. I am confident, in fact, that you are already partway there.

I hope, too, that my own personal journey has inspired you, and given you more confidence to follow your own. I hope the way ahead is clear now.

One of my biggest dreams was – and is – to be able to create a movement for people throughout the world. To help other people realize their dreams. To help you find the right path for you, and a deeper meaning in life.

When I started my business, there were many people who told me I would never succeed, but I kept the faith. I persevered – even when it hurt. I held on to my dream. I fell over again and again. My wife picked me up off the floor too many times to count, and made me keep following that dream.

Today that dream is a reality thanks to that very fact - that I held on to the dream.

You cannot go back and start from scratch in your life, but you can make the decision to create a new and different path forward. The important thing is not to stand still. To realize that everything around us, including ourselves, is in a state of constant change.

Use this book as a tool in life. Perhaps it makes sense to you today. Or perhaps you will read it again in 10 years´ time, and it will mean something entirely different. Whatever the case, I hope that your "The Life Bridge" will help you find balance in your life. And I hope, too, that you will keep your balance, so you don't let important things in life slip through your fingers, mistaking them for mere bagatelles. That you won't take anything for granted. That you won't lose focus on making active choices as well as active non-choices. Remember, too, that growth breeds growth. The things you dream of today – and things which you feel are important to you today – may not be important in a month's time, in a year, or in 10 years time. The relationship between you and your surroundings constantly changes, and so do your priorities.

When I was about 30, I told everyone that my ambition was to earn so much money that I could retire at 50. Today, my greatest dream is stay fit and healthy until I am at least 90 years old, so that for the rest of my life, I can carry on inspiring and helping others to grow. Create more happiness in the world and more freedom in humanity in general. In short, to carry on doing what I do, because I love what I do. As Steve Jobs said, *"The only way to do great work is to love what you do. If you haven't found it yet, keep looking. Don't settle."*

One of my greatest dreams is still to live in a world in which everyone has achieved a better balance in their lives. Where everyone can achieve that balance between happiness now and the beauty of dreaming for the future. A world in which we humans become better at stopping before it's too late. One in which we listen to ourselves and take greater care of ourselves. Where, together, we can make the world a better place tomorrow.

I would like to share a quotation with you, which has been a great source of inspiration to me during the last couple of years. The quotation is from the American rapper, Prince Ea.

"It is not death that most people fear. It´s the fear of waking up one day to find that we have never really lived the life we wanted."

I couldn´t agree more. And I try very hard to live my ideal life every day. Every day I try to inject some meaning into that day. I don´t wait until tomorrow. I let my feelings guide me, tell me what to dream of – and then I follow that, and believe in it. This is how I live my life, and it is has given me a deep sense of purpose in my life. Because the last thing I want to do is end up with a pile of regrets.

A number of studies have been conducted with the elderly who are dying, where they have been asked:

"Is there anything you wish you had done differently?"

Most people answered that they regretted the things they HADN´T done. Hadn´t achieved.

Therefore, let me ask you one last question:

Is there something you haven´t done yet? Is there something you haven´t achieved yet?

If the answer is yes, then my advice to you is:

Start Living Your Life. Your Life.

Live your life.

Follow your dreams.

You have been given a gift – use it.

I wish you all the best on your journey.

Ulrik

QUESTIONS/ EXERCISES

Chapter 1 - INTRODUCTION

- Notice what you dream about and ask yourself: What do I dream of most?
- Ask yourself the following questions: If there were no limits at all – what would I like to do with my life?
- Think about what freedom means to you.

Chapter 2 – WHAT ARE YOUR DREAMS?

- Try the following exercise. Take a piece of paper and write down what you would really like to do/have in your life versus all the things you don´t want. Compare the two lists. Which one is the longest?
- Think about the following over the next few days: Do you believe that what you think is what you´ll attract?
- Write down one of your dreams. Be specific about the details of the dream. Say it out loud. Notice how it feels to take responsibility for your dream.
- Begin to focus on the things you would like to have in your life, and reject thoughts of what you don´t want.

Chapter 3 – HOW DO YOU PRIORITIZE?

- Go for a long walk today and think about the following: Did I choose the life I am living? Actively?
- Make a list of your priorities – as they appear today – and as you would like them to be in the future.
- Find inspiration in "The Identity Leadership Model". Choose three areas to focus on in your life, and identify the extent to which you can feel that heart, energy and dreams are present in these three focus areas.
- Make a plan showing how you will develop your ILS to a higher level.

Chapter 4 – INSIGHT PROVIDES PERSPECTIVE

- Try and feel what or who you are most grateful for in your life.
- Be honest. Is there something or someone you really take for granted in your life?
- Cultivate silence today. Enjoy a day all by yourself. Unplug the phone, ignore your emails and disconnect the TV – and try and enjoy your own company instead – minus noise.
- Reflect on whether you are in a conscious or unconscious state.

Chapter 5 – YOU HAVE A CHOICE. NOW

- Think about the following: Do you choose to have freedom in your life now or do you reject it?
- Write down 5 things that represent ultimate freedom to you.
- Start telling yourself every single day, beginning from today that YOU make your own happiness in YOUR life. YOU are responsible for it, and you hold the key.

Chapter 6 – ON HABITS- AND HOW WE BREAK THEM

- Today you are going to examine your habits more closely: Which ones would you like to get rid of?
- Now give this some thought: Which new habits do you want to replace the old ones with?
- During the coming week, you must practice introducing at least one new habit into your daily routine.
- Try and perceive how other people view your good and not so good habits.

Chapter 7 - THE PLASTER EFFECT

- Be honest with yourself. Are you using plasters to cover up something in your life? Do you use something or someone to deaden the pain?
- Think about the following: Can you notice whether your heart is trying to tell you something?
- Write down three things that you know you feel deep down inside yourself, but which you have tried to suppress.

Chapter 8 – THE HEAD VS. THE HEART

- When did you last make a decision with your head instead of your heart?
- How did that feel?
- Did it make you happier? Calmer? Or perhaps frustrated deep down inside?
- Try to identify that feeling and write it down.

Chapter 9 – LISTEN TO YOUR HEART

- Today, listen to a heart meditation.
- Today, act exclusively based on your intuition.
- Today, be kind to your heart.
- Today is the day, when you take timeout and begin listening to your inner dialog. Would you talk to others the way you talk to yourself?

Chapter 10 – IT´S TIME TO RECAP – ARE YOU ALREADY BECOMING A LITTLE MORE CONSCIOUS?

- Ask yourself the following questions:
- Do I surround myself with the right people?
- Where am I headed in life?
- Do I use my time as I would really like to?
- Is what I say, what I do?
- Write down 10 things you are grateful for – right here and now.
- Take a sheet of paper. Write down your greatest dream. Then close your eyes. Imagine that you are on the way to achieving that dream. Imagine that it is about to be fulfilled.

Chapter 11- YOUR AUTHENTIC SELF

- Be honest. Do you have any behavioral patterns or reactions that are inappropriate when you can feel your emotions smoldering under the surface?
- Ask yourself: What is the worst that could happen if you dropped your outer façade and faced up to your inner conflict? Faced it head on. Would it be a little uncomfortable perhaps?
- Go for a walk in the woods today while you listen to some soothing, meditative music. Try and switch off your thoughts as much as you can.

Chapter 12 – USE YOUR INTUITION

- Try and get in touch with your own "gut feeling". What is it telling you to do today?
- Choose according to your intuition instead of your thoughts today: Do something you have never dared to do before.
- Before you fall asleep tonight notice: What feels different today compared to yesterday?

Chapter 13 – WHAT IS ENERGY?

- Today, you are going to do something that you know energizes you and makes you happy.
- Today, you should go for a run/go for a walk. Notice what you think about while you are out.
- Write down 5 things that you know fill you with terrific energy.

Chapter 14 - THE LIFE BRIDGE MODEL

- Work with your Life Bridge Model in depth today.
- Write down 5 things/people/circumstances you are grateful for in your current life. Write down which 5 dreams occupy your thoughts the most. Then compare the two lists:
- Are the two points in your life in balance – if not, how will you achieve this balance?

Chapter 15 – THE PATH TO VISUALIZATION

- Work intensively on one of your biggest dreams today.
- Visualize your dream by saying it out loud, writing it down, and by hanging up pictures and photos that represent your dream.
- Carry out at least 3 actions that will bring your dream a little closer to becoming a reality.

Chapter 16 – THE UNIVERSE IS LISTENING

- Think about how you would answer the following 3 questions:
- Do you have any dreams in your life that you have ignored so far – and if so, what are they?
- Do you feel that your intuition has your best interests at heart – or not?
- How do you feel when you listen to your inner voice?
- Do you remember to ask for help – and are you specific enough?

Chapter 17 – WHAT YOU SHOULD KNOW ABOUT TIME

- Take a closer look at how you use YOUR time.
- What is your attitude towards time?
- Do you feel that you use your time as you want to?
- Do you feel that you make the most of your time?
- Write down 5 things that you consider are a waste of your time – things where you would like to minimize the amount of time you spend on them in your life.

Chapter 18 – THE POWER IN ASKING FOR HELP

- Today, you are going to say what you wish for out loud, what you dream of, what your heart desires.
- Today, you are going to let yourself ask the Universe for help, to ask for something you would like.
- Today, you are going to do something that brings you closer to the universal energy – go for a walk near the ocean, close your eyes and listen to the birds, today let yourself think big thoughts about the universe which you are a part of.

Chapter 19 - CONNECTING THE DOTS

- Identify three areas in your life in which you are afraid to lose control.
- Think about the following: What would happen if you did lose control? Notice how this makes you feel. Initially, you will probably feel afraid. But how do you feel after this?
- Try and recall the dreams that might already have been fulfilled, and try to connect the elements (the dots) that all came together in the end to make that dream come true.

Chapter 20 – EVERYTHING IS CONNECTED

- Ask yourself the following questions:
- Are you 100% the same person at work vs. the person you are at home?
- How often must you compromise on being your authentic self?
- When are you really you?
- What needs to happen before you can be yourself all the time – in any situation?

Chapter 21 – YOU CAN MOVE THE PROCESS ALONG

- Practice your breathing technique today. Connect with your breathing.
- Connect with your inner calm and patience today. Repeat to yourself that you must have faith in your process.
- Think about the following: What or who is holding you back and preventing you from achieving your dream RIGHT NOW? Is it yourself?

Chapter 22 – LET´S CALL IT THE "PRINCIPLE" OF ATTRACTION

- Dedicate today to your dreams and these three principles.
- Get right to the heart of your dreams and examine them in depth using these three steps:
- The Principle of Quality
- The Principle of Intensity
- The Principle of Attraction

As time goes by, your priorities will also change, so remember to work with THE PRINCIPLE OF ATTRACTION on a continual basis. Stand in front of the mirror and repeat: I am the most important person in my life." Notice how this feels. Repeat this exercise regularly until this feeling becomes a part of you.

www.ingramcontent.com/pod-product-compliance
Lightning Source LLC
Chambersburg PA
CBHW071622080526
44588CB00010B/1224